IMPROVING ACCESS TO LIBRARY RESOURCES:

The Influence of Organization of Library Collections, and of User Attitudes Toward Innovative Services

by

Richard M. Dougherty

and

Laura L. Blomquist

The Scarecrow Press, Inc.
Metuchen, N.J.   1974

This work was prepared under a National Science Foundation grant (#32381).

Library of Congress Cataloging in Publication Data

Dougherty, Richard M
  Improving access to library resources.

  1. Libraries, University and college--United States.
2. Universities and colleges--United States--Faculty.
3. Library use studies. 4. Research. I. Blomquist,
Laura L., joint author. II. Title.
Z675.U5D 58   027.7'0973   73-20482
ISBN 0-8108-0637-1

Copyright 1974 by Richard M. Dougherty
and Laura L. Blomquist

TABLE OF CONTENTS

	Page
Foreword, by Roger C. Greer	vii
Preface	ix
Acknowledgments	xi
Chapter I. Introduction	1
Chapter II. Methodology of the Investigation	6
Samples	8
Interview Guides	13
Classed Interest Profiles	16
Classification Process	16
Limitations of Interest Profiles	22
Shelf List Count of Document Dispersion Pattern	23
Distance Measurements	27
Special Evaluation Measurements	28
Summary	28
Chapter III. Results of the Study	31
Library Use and Dispersion of Materials	31
Dispersion of Holdings and Users' Expectation Rate	43
Library Use and Distance	44
Expectation Ratings of Library Users	47
Expectation Rates of Syracuse University Faculty	47
Comparison of SU and OSU Faculty Expectation Rates	49
Evaluation of the Document Delivery Service	54
Accessibility of Materials in a Document Delivery Environment	54
Value of Delivery Service to OSU Faculty	55

	Attitudes Toward Document Delivery During a Period of Tight Budgets	57
	Document Delivery and Changes in Perceived Importance of the Library as a Source of Information	58
	Comparison of SU and OSU Faculty Attitudes Toward Delivery Systems	60
	OSU Non-user Attitudes Toward Delivery	62
	Summary	64
Chapter IV.	Other Findings of the Investigation	67
	Library Use and Teaching	67
	Departmental Reading Rooms	69
	Who Retrieves Materials From the Library?	70
	Changing Faculty Research Interests	72
	Doctoral Students in the Role of Communications Gate Keepers	73
	Summary	74
Chapter V.	Findings, Conclusions and Implications	76
	Library Users and the Dispersion of Materials	76
	User Attitudes Toward Library Effectiveness: Expectation Ratings	79
	Comparison Between Users' and Non-Users' Attitudes Toward Document Delivery	81
	Users' Attitudes Toward an Innovative Library Service: Document Delivery	82
	Innovation Diffusion	83
	The Role of the Library in the Teaching Program	84
	Faculty Retrieval of Library Materials	84
	Doctoral Students as Communication Gate Keepers	85
	Summary	85

Appendices

A - 1	Syracuse University Appointment Phone Call	88

A - 2	Syracuse University Interview Instrument	89
A - 3	Tabulations for SU Interviews	93
B - 1	Instructions for Shelf List Count of Document Dispersion Patterns at the Library Processing Center	116
B - 2	Document Dispersion Pattern Worksheet	118
B - 3	Shelf List Count of Document Dispersion Patterns--Explanation	120
B - 4	Shelf List Count of Document Dispersion Patterns	134
B - 5	Ranges Derived from Document Dispersion Patterns	139
B - 6	Summary of Means by Group and Department: Library Holding Documents, Library Used, Document Exposure Index, and Expectation Rate	140
B - 7	Document Exposure Index: Frequency Distribution	143
B - 8	Relationship Between DEI and Library Used First--Branch vs No Branches	144
B - 9	Ranking of ER Means by Department with Document Exposure Index	145
C - 1	Distance Ranges of Libraries Respondents Ranked	146
C - 2	Distance Ranges of Libraries Used and Not Used	147
C - 3	Percent Holdings and Distance of Library	148
D - 1	Ohio State University Interview Guide I	149
D - 2	Tabulations for OSU Guide I	154
E - 1	Ohio State University Interview Guide II	168
E - 2	Tabulations for OSU Guide II	171
Index		177

FOREWORD

It has been almost a hundred years since the academic library acquired its present role in the instructional and research processes of higher education. It was near the beginning of the fourth quarter of the nineteenth century that research became recognized as a significant activity of the academician. Johns Hopkins University, founded in 1876, was launched with the German model of research and graduate education as the dominant function of the University.*
In this environment the library was thrust into focus as a fundamental component in the accomplishment of these new objectives of scholarship.

While collection-building had long been the primary function of the library, university administrators were also invoking such phrases as the "heart of the university" to mask the reality of benign neglect. While the library was essentially a passive storage center of book treasures and archives, there was no serious concern about its peripheral position in institutional budgets. The new scholarship brought changes which began to give substance to the grand phrases about the library. The librarian, happy with his new responsibility and added prestige, advanced on his task of collection-building with a zest and vigor that maintained momentum for most of a century. His other responsibility of making his collections available for use never achieved a significance in his daily concern equal to the problems of acquiring material. Indeed, the prestige of an academic library is measured primarily by the size of its collections. The organization of the library was primarily a consequence of growth. On the one hand, the expansion of the parent institution and physical disbursement of academic units forced the library to decentralize some of its collections.

---

*Rothstein, Samuel. "The context of reference service: The rise of research and research libraries, 1850-1900," in Harris, Michael, ed. Reader in American Library History. Washington, D.C.: NCR, 1971, p. 198.

At the same time, the rapid growth of the library collections produced the same pressure from inside the library. Lack of stack space in the central library made opting for a decentralized system more palatable. With each new generation of central library building came a coincidental effort to bring many far-flung departmental enterprises back into the central library fold. For the most part during the past century, organizational decisions have rarely reflected the actual needs of library users. That is, these decisions were not likely to be based on systematically collected and analyzed empirical data regarding user behavior patterns.

Recently, the library administrator's attention shifted from the former preoccupation with collection-building to better means of making the collections more accessible at times, places, quantities, and levels appropriate to the needs of people. Some of this is due to the advent of new technologies which can be employed to manipulate large data bases. A consequence of this has been the promotion of inquiry in other areas of the library's responsibilities and objectives.

The present study adds another link in the growing chain of evidence on the attitudes and behavior patterns of a specific group of library users--the faculty. The central thrust of this study is on the attitudes of faculty regarding the library's document delivery capacity for them. These attitudes are probed in a context of a departmental and central library organizational pattern. An external measure of the validity of these attitudes has been achieved by a comparison of subject resources against subject interest. The conclusions found in earlier research that convenience and ease of access are of a primary concern is reaffirmed here. However, this study also concludes that decentralization is not the answer to increasing user access and satisfaction. The suggestion is made that means other than library organization (e.g., a delivery service) must be exploited in order to achieve greater faculty satisfaction and use of academic library services.

ROGER C. GREER

PREFACE

The motivation for this investigation derived from a series of visits to institutions which were deeply committed to the design, development, and operation of non-traditional automated information systems. At the time of the visits, the systems seemed to be working technically but, paradoxically, they did not appear to have made a significant impact on the respective user communities. Although few people associated with the systems openly expressed concern, there were non-verbal indicators which suggested that some people were becoming nervous. Since all of the systems represented high expenditures of time and money, a feeling of uneasiness seemed quite appropriate.

The question which intrigued the investigator was why users had not shown a greater receptivity. The reactions of the users interviewed were not negative, although some users were not convinced that the new system was superior to their current information-gathering procedures. One did not have to look far to develop a hypothesis. Users of innovative information systems had reacted like anyone else who is confronted with a new idea, product or service: he must first be convinced that the new idea will be of sufficient benefit to him in order to motivate a change in his behavior.

Another problem which grew out of the interviews with users focused attention on the difficulties and frustration they experienced in trying to obtain documents. The new systems seemed to have created a systems imbalance. Citations are now much easier to obtain than the documents themselves. Obviously, we must improve our ability to provide documents before the systems imbalance can be corrected.

Because there is a need to improve our document delivery capabilities in libraries, it seemed appropriate to the investigator to consider the relationship between a researcher in an academic environment and the location of materials potentially of interest to him. Specifically, can he locate them? Is he willing to generate the effort to search for materials? What would be his reaction to an improved delivery capability? Would an improvement in document accessibility have an affect on his attitudes toward the library? It was with these questions in mind that the current investigation was undertaken.

RICHARD M. DOUGHERTY

ACKNOWLEDGMENTS

The authors owe debts of gratitude to many individuals and organizations. It was a Council on Library Resources Fellowship awarded to one of the investigators, Richard M. Dougherty, which enabled him to gather information about innovative library systems. The current project is a direct result of the CLR Fellowship. The authors are particularly grateful to the National Science Foundation for supporting the research reported here under Grant Number 32381.

The authors wish to thank the Syracuse University Library for granting access to their union shelf list. It was a particularly difficult time for the Library because preparations were being made for a move into a new building. We are particularly appreciative of the cooperation we received from Mr. Warren Boes, Mr. Max Willocks, Mrs. Indra David, Mrs. Theresa Strozik, and Mrs. Gina Wu.

The interviews of users of the Ohio State University Library delivery system could not have been conducted without the cooperation and support of the OSU Library administration, Mr. Hugh Atkinson and Mr. Larry X. Besant, and several staff members from the Library's Circulation Department.

The investigation proved to be a difficult undertaking because it was completed within a very tight time-frame. There were many separate tasks to coordinate in a very short period of time. We are particularly indebted to Mr. Morrell D. Boone, who served as the project's faculty associate and participated in all of the faculty interviews; Dr. Roger C. Greer, who encouraged the project as Dean of the School of Library Science, and who later provided a valuable critique of the final report; Mr. John C. Allen, who provided the team with sage advice concerning the construction of the faculty subject profiles; and Mr. William E. McGrath, who was responsible for the mathematical analyses.

Three graduate students from the School of Library

Science, Kathleen Sands, Karlye Gill and June Brower, took time off from their regular studies to assist in the preparation of the faculty subject-interest profiles. During the months of March and April, 1972, several additional students joined them at the Syracuse University Library processing center to develop the document dispersion patterns--an especially tedious task and one where accuracy was of prime importance. Those who worked with us were: Marianne Cassell, Kathleen Allen, John Bennett, The Lam, David Trithart and Helene Shrier.

Finally, the authors wish to thank Linda Lagua who served as the project's administrative assistant. In her quiet manner and always with a smile, she handled a multitude of tasks with speed and efficiency.

Richard M. Dougherty
Laura L. Blomquist

Chapter I

INTRODUCTION

Academic libraries have traditionally functioned as passive service agencies; that is, they have served people who have initiated the effort to receive their services, but have made little effort to seek out those who may have information needs but who have not sought satisfaction in libraries. Such practices have contributed toward perpetuating the stereotyped image of the library as a storehouse of the records of mankind. Now, technology has provided us with new opportunities. Users no longer need to rely solely on printed sources of information. They can now retrieve bibliographical information from computer terminals located in the sanctuary of their departments and even their offices. Despite these new systems, the difficulties commonly associated with document retrieval, long a frustration to researchers, have not been eliminated. The problem, then, is to develop more effective strategies of delivery to match users with documents; because, as bibliographic data become more easily accessible, the pressures to develop better delivery systems will mount. Unfortunately, the complexity of the challenge becomes readily apparent when one reviews the typical university library system and campus environment.

The large campus is highly decentralized in terms of schools, departments, faculty, students and libraries. Intracampus transportation is not always convenient to a user who must borrow materials from more than one branch within the library system. In addition, proliferating interdisciplinary institutes and study groups have separated users further from materials. Users seem to be unable to find their way through the maze of library records and shelves of books. Understandably, though regrettably, their frustrations are frequently vented upon the library staff, resulting in an aura of antipathy between patrons and librarians.

Although one frequently reads that more must be

learned about the information use habits of researchers, in fact, a great deal is known about how researchers obtain information. Slater found that the distance from a researcher's office to the library he typically frequents influences his use of that library.[1] Likewise, Ennis stated that, with public library users, availability affects what is read.[2] Berelson reported in 1949 that a survey based on a national sample revealed that one-half of the public library's adult users lived within a mile of the public library.[3] Allen and Rosenberg found that information channels are selected on the basis of convenience rather than on the amount of information those channels are expected to provide.[4,5]

A study conducted at the University of Michigan revealed that, although the faculty disliked the dispersion of materials among departmental libraries, they did not want to merge their own department library with the main library.[6] Voigt, Hanson and Flowers all stressed the importance of personal contacts to scientists in their information quest.[7,8,9] Hanson estimated from his studies that personal contacts satisfied between twenty-five and fifty percent of a researcher's information needs. These findings support the concept of the invisible college described by Price in his study, <u>Little Science, Big Science</u>.[10]

If these behavioral characteristics are applicable to the researcher in an academic setting, then it should be possible to hypothesize a behavioral pattern for the typical academic researcher, regardless of discipline. He will gather much of his information from the sources which are most convenient to him. Therefore, he probably will rely heavily on his personal collection, and he will seek information from his colleagues; those within his own department first, then via telephone from professional acquaintances located elsewhere. Because convenience, proximity and accessibility are not necessarily related to the yield of information sources, it is reasonable to assume that a researcher may not have accessible to him the most relevant data to meet his information needs. Moreover, unless a researcher is highly motivated, it is not likely that he will use all of the libraries on campus which house documents relevant to his needs. He will tend to use those libraries which are most accessible to him. In short, if the source is not easily accessible, he will not use it.

The investigators assumed in this study that the

Introduction

attitudes exhibited by users toward the library may be as important as, or even more important than, actual library effectiveness. Or, stated in other terms, if a user believes that the library is effective, then for him the library is effective. Conversely, if a user believes the library is ineffective, then for him it is ineffective. For example, even if a university library could retrieve one hundred percent of the documents specifically requested by researchers, if in the researcher's mind the library is an inaccessible, inconvenient source, he is likely to turn to alternative channels for his information.

The traditional solution of academic librarians to the problem of improving accessibility has been to establish specialized subject libraries in close proximity to academic teaching and research units. Although decentralization has ameliorated the problem to a certain degree, these library systems are expensive to maintain. Now, during this period of shrinking budgets and rising costs, further decentralization does not appear a viable managerial alternative. We must identify other options to provide solutions.

The investigators formulated the following hypotheses in order to study the influence of campus library organizational structure on the document delivery effectiveness of the library:

1. That within the context of traditional library and information systems, there may be an irreconcilable separation between the physical location of informational sources and the persons who require information.

2. That, in a period dominated by interdisciplinary studies, traditional decentralized (i.e., departmental branches) library systems do not offer researchers easy accessibility to potentially relevant information.

3. That decentralized systems neither increase user satisfaction nor achieve a high utilization of information resources.

4. That an academic library system could increase user satisfaction based on users' perceptions of the library, and achieve greater utilization of its resources through the introduction of some type of document delivery system.

To sum up, the general thrusts of this investigation

were to probe faculty attitudes toward library effectiveness, the effect of dispersion of resources on these attitudes, and whether or not document delivery systems produce changes in user attitudes toward the library. The first objective was to identify the relationship between the location of researchers and (1) the location of documents of potential interest to the researcher in the institution's official library system; (2) the degree of physical dispersion of relevant documents within that library system; and (3) the distance from each researcher's primary working office to the relevant documents. The second objective was to measure researchers' expectations that they can successfully find materials in the library when searching on their own, and to compare these expectation levels with the expectations of researchers working in an environment where documents are delivered to them. Document delivery systems were considered as one means to improve accessibility; consequently, the third objective was to measure user attitudes toward delivery services in two contrasting campus environments, one with and one without the service.

Notes

1. Slater, M., "Types of use and user in industrial libraries; some impressions." Journal of Documentation, Vol. 19, No. 1 (March, 1963), pp. 2-16.

2. Ennis, P. H., "Adult book reading in the United States." (National Opinion Research Center, 1965, Report No. 105).

3. Berelson, B., The Library's Public. New York: Columbia University Press, 1949, pp. 43-6.

4. Allen, T. J., "Organizational aspects of information flow and technology; with discussion." ASLIB Proceedings, Vol. 20 (November 20, 1968), pp. 433-54.

5. Rosenberg, V., "Factors affecting the preferences of industrial personnel for information gathering methods." Information Storage and Retrieval Journal, Vol. 3 (July, 1967), pp. 119-27.

6. University of Michigan Survey Research Center, "Faculty Appraisal of a University Library, Ann Arbor, Michigan." University of Michigan University Library, 15 December 1961, in Bates, Marcia J., User Studies:

A Review for Librarians and Information Scientists, (March, 1971), ED 047738, p. 38.

7. Voigt, M. J., "A researcher and his sources of scientific information." LIBRI, Vol. 9, No. 3 (1959), pp. 177-93.

8. Hanson, C. W., "Research on users' needs: where is it getting us?" ASLIB Proceedings, Vol. 16 (February, 1964), pp. 64-78.

9. Flowers, D. H., "Reasons for the variations in the information needs of scientists." Journal of Documentation, Vol. 21, No. 2 (June, 1965), pp. 83-112.

10. Price, Derrick John de Solla, Little Science, Big Science. New York: Columbia University Press, 1963.

Chapter II

METHODOLOGY OF THE INVESTIGATION

The investigators were faced with the problem of collecting information from two samples of university faculty who were users of two library systems with distinguishing characteristics. Both libraries, of course, are decentralized organizationally; and both shared to a varying degree the financial problems of the current fiscal crunch. At the time of the study, however, the Syracuse University library system was preparing to move out of an archaic central facility to the new $13 million Ernest Stevenson Bird Library which would absorb several of the branch libraries. It was also in the process of converting from a manual system to an on-line circulation system and was preparing a computer-based shelf list for the move to the new building. The Ohio State University libraries, on the other hand, had introduced an on-line circulation system about eighteen months before, and document delivery service for monographs about twelve months before the investigators arrived on campus. Change is disconcerting in itself; and needless to say, the on-going and pending changes at SU and OSU have influenced faculty attitudes toward both library systems.

In fact, the primary purpose of the team's visit to OSU was to explore the reaction of delivery system users to that service. It would have been preferable to conduct a before/after study of faculty attitudes toward the delivery service and the library to determine if changes in attitude occurred. Because that was impossible, the investigators hoped to obtain an indication of how and if attitudes changed, by comparing the attitudes of SU researchers who were without delivery service and those of OSU researchers who had used such a service.

Before proceeding, it might be beneficial to describe briefly the operation of the Ohio State University delivery service. When an individual wants a specific document, he

Methodology

simply has to pick up the phone in his office or home and place his request with operators who man the on-line terminals at the main library. Requests may also be transmitted through branch libraries. Once requests are received, trained library staff search to locate the ordered documents and send them through campus mail. Judging from those interviewed, the time-span from request to delivery ranged from a day to a week. Most faculty attributed delays to campus mail rather than to the library. Several subjects did complain, however, that there was no systematic procedure of notification when a document could not be delivered immediately because it was signed out, on reserve or lost. Frequently, the on-line circulation system fed back information on the status of the monograph before the researcher hung up the phone. Most of the interviewees were very positive about such feedback and the investigators found it almost impossible to distinguish between user enthusiasm for the automated system and enthusiasm for the delivery service. In fact, on a few occasions during interviews, the investigators had to note that there was a distinction and that one service was quite feasible without the other. Generally, the on-line circulation system and delivery service make it possible for users to eliminate the trip to the library to search the card catalog and the stacks, to avoid the charge-out process, and, finally, the task of lugging several books back to their offices. The user must have a fairly firm idea of what he wants, since subject searches are presently all but unavailable on the on-line system. In other words, neither the delivery service nor the computerized system eliminates completely the need to go to the library.

To gather data at SU, the research team employed several techniques: personal interviews, subject interest-profiling, shelf list location counts, distance measurements, and two special evaluative measurements developed to gauge library and user effectiveness.

The methodology employed was designed to draw out faculty reaction to both library systems as a whole, as well as reactions to a document delivery service. It was also structured to relate the holdings of the library system with the individual's teaching and research interests in order to determine what effect, if any, library organization and distance had on an individual's library use patterns.

SAMPLES

Syracuse University. The interview sample was drawn from 970 faculty members: individuals holding academic appointments at the ranks of lecturers, instructors, assistant professors, associate professors and professors. Graduate teaching assistants and research associates without faculty rank were excluded from the original population. Because no shelf list data were attainable for the profiles, faculty of the Schools of Law and Nursing were also eliminated from the original population.

A ten percent sample of one hundred faculty was pulled from a computer-generated print-out of the faculty. Faculty were numbered from one to 970 and a random number table was used to make the sample selection. More than one hundred numbers were drawn; numbers over one hundred were used to replace individuals who were unavailable for interviews. In all, nineteen subjects were dropped: eight who were on leave of absence; seven who had terminated their affiliation with SU; two who refused to participate; and two who were not familiar with the library system--a blind professor and a visiting professor with no instructional duties. Table 1 summarizes the percent of the SU sample by department relative to the total faculty. Table 2 indicates the academic rank distribution of sample members.

Table 1. SU SAMPLE RELATED TO TOTAL FACULTY BY DEPARTMENTAL AFFILIATION

Department	Percent of sample	Percent of total faculty
Afro-American Studies	0	1.0
Air Force, ROTC	2	0.4
Army, ROTC	1	0.5
School of Architecture	3	2.8
School of Education	7	9.6
College of Engineering	9	10.5
College of Human Development	6	5.4
School of Management	5	5.8
School of Library Science	1	1.1
School of Public Communications	2	3.3
College of Visual & Performing Arts	13	10.7

Department	Percent of sample	Percent of total faculty
School of Social Work	6	2.9
Systems and Information Science	0	1.9
Anthropology	3	1.4
Biology	2	3.2
Chemistry	4	2.2
Classics	0	0.3
Economics	3	1.8
English	4	3.3
Fine Arts	2	1.1
Geography	3	1.2
Geology	0	1.0
German	1	0.7
History	7	3.1
Mathematics	1	4.5
Philosophy	2	1.4
Physical Education, men	0	0.6
Physical Education, women	0	1.3
Physics	1	3.1
Political Science	3	3.2
Psychology	4	3.3
Citizenship & Public Affairs	0	0.5
Religion	2	1.4
Romance Languages	1	2.4
Science Teaching	1	0.5
Slavic Languages	0	0.4
Social Science Program	0	0.4
Sociology	1	1.6
	100	100.0

Table 2. SU FACULTY INTERVIEWED CATEGORIZED BY ACADEMIC RANK

Rank	f
Full Professor	23
Associate Professor	22
Assistant Professor	40
Instructor	6
Lecturer	9
Total	100

For purposes of selected analyses, the SU departments were grouped into three broad categories: Science, Social Science and Humanities, as shown in Table 3.

Table 3. CLASSIFICATION OF ACADEMIC DEPARTMENTS BY GROUPS

Group I Sciences	Group II Social Sciences	Group III Humanities
Air Force	Air Force	Architecture
Biology	Anthropology	English
Chemistry	Army, ROTC	Fine Arts
Engineering	Economics	German
Mathematics	Education	Human Development
Physics	Geography	Library Science
Psychology	History	Philosophy
Science Teaching	Human Development	Religion
Human Development	Management	Romance Languages
	Political Science	Visual & Performing Arts
	Public Communications	
	Social Work	
	Sociology	

As shown in Table 3, members of two departments, Air Force and Human Development, were assigned to different groups on the basis of their research and teaching interests. Because one Air Force professor's emphasis was in management, he was included in the social science group, whereas the second's emphasis was in aeronautics, placing him in the science grouping. Members selected from the department of Human Development were assigned to all three groups: one specialist in nutrition to the sciences; one each specializing in preschool education, child development and the family in the social sciences; and two concentrating in design and the arts in humanities.

Ohio State University. The OSU subjects interviewed were known users of the campus library delivery service, and were contacted by OSU personnel before the project team arrived on the OSU campus. Phone calls to set up interviews resulted in appointments with 57 out of 120 known users of the delivery service. The other 63 either did not

Methodology 11

answer their phones or were out of town during the week the team was on campus. The sample population was limited because it is OSU's policy not to maintain a record of users in order to assure user privacy. In fact, special permission was obtained from the Library Advisory Committee before the library released the names of recent users.

Table 4. DEPARTMENTAL AFFILIATIONS OF INTERVIEWEES
OHIO STATE UNIVERSITY

Department	f
I. Users of the Delivery Service	
Agricultural Economics	3
Agricultural Engineering	1
Allied Medicine	1
Anthropology	1
Chemistry	1
Computer Science	1
Design	2
East Asian Language & Literature	1
Engineering	2
English	6
Finance	1
Food Science & Nutrition	1
History	7
History of Art	1
Home Economics	2
Law	2
Mathematics	1
Music	1
Natural Resources	1
Nursing	2
Optometry	1
Pharmacology	1
Political Science	2
Psychology	2
Romance Languages	2
Social Work	1
Sociology	1
Speech Communications	1
Others	10
	59

Department	f
II. Non-users of the Delivery Service	
Anatomy	1
Classics	1
Dairy Science	1
Economics	1
Entomology	1
Geology	1
Microbiology	1
Nursing	1
	8

Table 5. OSU FACULTY INTERVIEWED CATEGORIZED BY ACADEMIC RANK

Rank	f	%		
Full Professor	12	20	Others	
Associate Professor	5	8	Adm. assistant	2
Assistant Professor	14	24	Student - staff	4
Instructor	8	14	Research associate	4
Lecturer	1	2	Teaching associate	3
Others	18	30	Fellow	2
Unknown	1	2	Directors of support services	2
	59	100	Program supervisor	1
				18

The OSU sample was not randomly selected and comprised less than one percent of the total faculty. Despite its non-random character, sample members were distributed among many academic departments (Table 4) and were fairly well distributed among faculty ranks (Table 5). Inadvertently, some non-professional staff were also included in the sample, and Table 5 also shows a breakdown of their responsibilities. Obviously, the sample cannot be construed as representative of the more than 5000 faculty on campus; therefore, no definitive conclusions may be drawn from the results of the interviews. Nonetheless, the investigators felt that the attitudes reflected by the OSU subjects are an indication of the attitudes held by users of the delivery service.

Methodology 13

During the last day, the team interviewed ten nonusers, all full professors, to sense out their attitudes toward document delivery and their reasons for not using the service.* Because the phone calls were made the day before, only ten out of 60 people could be contacted for interviews the next morning. Again, sample members were distributed among different departments (Table 4). Two of the "non-users" were found to be infrequent users of the delivery service; consequently, they were added to the original OSU user group, bringing the sample size to 59.

INTERVIEW GUIDES

The research team developed three structured guides to interview faculty at Syracuse University and Ohio State University (See Appendices A-2, D-1, and E-1). The telephone explanation the project's secretary used to set up the one hundred appointments at SU can be found in Appendix A-1.

Syracuse University Guide. The SU form was finalized after a pilot study of twelve faculty who were already excluded from the test sample. All three team members who would be interviewing at SU and OSU took part in the pilot study in order to distinguish between ambiguities and inconsistencies in question design and interviewer's technique. They met two or three times to practice interviewing and to discuss specific problems encountered in the pilot study in order to standardize the interview procedure as much as possible. Throughout the interviewing period at SU, the three interviewers kept each other informed on pertinent problems and techniques which arose in specific interviews.

Ohio State University Guide. The instrument for OSU was based on the SU guide and a questionnaire used to evaluate a delivery service at the University of Colorado[11] (See Appendix D-1). Ohio State library staff had already made appointments by phone with sample members when the team arrived on campus. With only four days on site, no pretest was possible; but after the first morning of interviewing, the

---

*Because the sample of OSU users contained so many junior ranks, the investigators specifically asked the library to contact only those with the rank of Professor. The objective was to learn if any notable differences in attitudes could be detected. The results are presented later in the study.

investigators compared notes to smooth out possible problem areas before continuing with the afternoon appointments.

The second guide devised for OSU was used to query non-users of the delivery service. It varies only slightly from the primary OSU instrument, but it delved into non-users' knowledge of the existence of a delivery service, their reasons for not using it, and a comparison of delivery service users' and non-users' attitudes toward the library. Needless to say, with such a small number of interviewees (eight), the results could have no weight on the conclusions. At best, they may serve as a pretest for a future in-depth comparison of users with non-users.

Rationale for Personal Interviews. The personal interview technique was adopted to allow investigators to probe the reasons behind specific answers and to follow up on interesting and unexpected comments elicited from the interviewees. In addition, the complexity of a few questions might have discouraged a thoughtful response if the subject had been queried by phone or by mailed questionnaire. The latter technique rarely produces a reliable return, and the project team did not have the time to wait for forthcoming replies. When setting up the interviews by phone, many faculty suggested that they were not "good" subjects because they did not "read books" or "rarely" used the library. The fact of the matter was that they did need and often obtained information from the library system but perhaps not in monograph form. The skillful interviewer could easily overcome such resistance by structuring the definition of "item" in the very first question: "Do you usually go to the library yourself to get a specific item?" For example, if the subject was in the visual and performing arts department, the interviewer would include in his description of "item" such terms as "slides," "art prints," "films," "scores" and/or "recordings," as well as the more traditional books and journals.

Another reason for using the personal interview technique and for setting specific appointments with sample members was to assure that the collected data would be reasonably representative of the Syracuse faculty as a whole. It is a relatively easy matter for an efficient secretary to put off callers who want to interview by phone or to drop an annoying questionnaire form in the circular file. Actually, when asked for an appointment, faculty were most cooperative when they were told that the study was a National Science

Methodology 15

Foundation project and when they were asked to set a specific time for the interview. Only four callbacks were necessary to complete the one hundred interviews. Thus, neither the subjects' time nor the investigators' time was squandered on needless waiting and repeated trips.

<u>Contents of Interview Guides</u>. In general, the SU and OSU interview instruments were developed to glean data on how and where faculty obtain information; the relative importance of different information sources; faculty use and the importance of departmental reading rooms; faculty's expectation of successfully locating desired documents from the library system; and finally, attitudes toward a faculty and graduate student document delivery service. Most of the specific questions in the guides are self-explanatory, but some comment is warranted on three. Question ten on the SU guide (See Appendix A-2), which explored library use in relation to faculty's instructional responsibilities, was added after the pilot study suggested possible "avoidance behavior"; that is, it appeared that they actively sought alternatives--paperbacks, collected materials, folders of xeroxed materials, etc.--to student use of the library system. Question nineteen, SU (See Appendix A-2), and questions twenty-one and twenty-two, OSU (See Appendix D-1), which compared current teaching and past publications with current research interests, were also added when several pilot study subjects indicated their fields of interest had completely changed in the last few years.

Finally, questions eleven and twelve, SU, and questions fifteen and sixteen, OSU, explored faculty sources of information. The investigators asked those interviewed at both SU and OSU to rate, either as important or unimportant, eight sources of information. The choices included: (1) personal collections, (2) university library system, (3) doctoral students, (4) conversations with colleagues on campus, (5) papers presented and heard at meetings, (6) departmental reading rooms, (7) conversations with colleagues off campus, and (8) colleagues' collections. Subjects were next asked to rank in order of importance those sources which they had noted as important to them. The question was not included either to define the sources faculty used to obtain information or to determine the relative importance of various sources. Its primary purpose was to determine if there was any difference in faculty attitudes toward the library in the two different environments--delivery and non-delivery service library systems.

CLASSED INTEREST PROFILES

Faculty interest profiles were constructed by adopting the idea of classifying courses as described by McGrath and Durand.[12] The purpose was to translate research and teaching interests of individual faculty into LC classification numbers which could then be related to the holdings of the library system, and specifically to the dispersion of these holdings throughout the system. The final interest profile for each individual consisted of LC class numbers derived from (1) the course description of the subjects he taught, (2) his reported current research interests, and (3) his publications of the last five years.

Profile Cards. As soon as the sample was drawn, graduate students began compiling profile cards by checking the 1971-72 fall and spring semesters' class schedules for courses taught by each respondent, and by cutting and pasting the course descriptions from the university catalogs on 5" x 8" cards. Each individual was represented by at least one such card, identified by his sample number, department notation and faculty rank. It was necessary to make several phone calls to departmental offices to obtain complete information for some data cards. After the subject was interviewed, the cards had to be updated by adding or subtracting courses, research interests and LC subject numbers for publications.

CLASSIFICATION PROCESS

Classification of Courses. A trial classification project was conducted by a professional librarian with some consultation with faculty colleagues. The trial project consisted of the classification of 15 courses taught by five different sample members. On the basis of the trial project, the investigators were able to construct guidelines to assist a classifier in determining which subjects were represented in each course and the level of specificity to be assigned. The guidelines were as follows:

1. Admit a fairly broad range of class numbers in different subject fields if there appears to be evidence of an interdisciplinary approach to course topics.

2. Do not limit the number of LC classification numbers assigned per course. Any and all considered appli-

cable, including long spans, such as TA800-901, should be included in the profile.

3. Survey courses should be classified, usually with long spans, to include any subtopics listed in available syllabi.

4. LC class numbers may be duplicated as often as necessary to provide a full profile. No class number is considered the exclusive property of any one individual or academic department. In fact, the trend toward interdisciplinary studies requires the multiple assignment of specific class numbers.

5. Be sure to include all relevant LC numbers for periodicals in each subject field of interest for each individual.

Following the completion of the test classification project and the development of guidelines for the classification of courses, three advanced graduate students in library science were instructed in the process of classifying courses taught by the sample researchers.

Where course descriptions were replete with topics covered, classifiers used an indexing technique, attempting to assign an LC subject number for each key word noted in the description. For example, the following Air Force, ROTC course description was relatively simple to classify:

AEROSPACE STUDIES: AEROSPACE OPERATIONS

ASC 415 and 416. Aerospace Operations. (1) and (1)

Study of meteorological data, atmospheric patterns, and other related weather phenomena affecting aerospace operations; navigational techniques, cartographic presentations, air-ground communications procedures, and other related rules governing aerospace operations.

Initially, the following LC numbers were assigned for the course:

UG 467, "Military meteorology"
? UG 470, "Military surveying, topography and mapping"

UG 630-670, "Military aeronautics"
? TA 597, "Surveying, applications of astronomy"
TL 556-558, "Aeronautics, meteorological"
TL 586-588, "Air navigation. Astronomy and navigation"
? TL 589-589.7, "Aeronautics instruments"
TL 692-697, "Communications and equipment, aeronautics"
GA 109, "Aerial cartography"
? G 142, "Aerial geography"

** KF 2400-2418, "Aviation, regulations, federal"

The above subject numbers also serve to illustrate some of the judgments necessary in developing a profile. The "?" preceding four of the numbers indicated the classifier questioned the appropriateness of the class designation. Two numbers, UG 470 and TA 597, were cut from the profile. The other two were judged to be relevant as a result of additional information gleaned from reading lists or other supplementary sources. The "**" number should have been included in the profile because the course does include federal regulations covering air operations. The information was revealed during the personal interview and came too late to be included in the shelf list count at the Library processing center.

To handle the more typical enigmatic course descriptions, the researchers used several techniques:

1. LC numbers from a professor's reading lists, when available, were noted and included in the profile. Such numbers frequently gave classifiers clues of entry into an area or range in the LC schedules. It should be noted that any LC subject number derived from a reading list or list of publications that had been assigned by university library catalogers and entered into the main catalog was considered a "hard" number. They were entered in ink on the profile cards and always included in the final edited profile.

2. Questions #17-19 of the SU interview guide were designed to glean additional data for the classifiers. Reading lists, syllabi, personal publications and vita sheets were all requested both at the time the appointment was set up and again by the researcher at the end of the interview. Many respondents had the material ready for the interviewers, although few respondents had everything available. Again, lists

Methodology 19

frequently produced "hard" numbers for the profile as well as needed specific data by which to classify course descriptions.

    3. The interview concluded with the researcher discussing specific questions related to the profile compilation. Because the LC classification scheme for literature assigns numbers for specific authors by type of work--prose and poetry--classifiers had to know which authors were covered in a course before assigning specific subject numbers. To classify a course titled "Economic Problems of Metropolitan Areas" required information concerning the specific problems. In short, the interviewer not only confirmed and updated the course listing for each respondent, but frequently, he obtained the basic information needed to assign subject numbers.

    Such procedures tended to validate or invalidate LC numbers already assigned to detailed course descriptions and made it possible to come up with LC numbers for such courses as "History 715," "Readings in Twentieth Century America" or "Afro-American History"; the latter deals with the study of urban poor in Syracuse, their culture and community. In addition, such collateral information revealed an individual's propensity, or lack thereof, for an interdisciplinary approach to his subject and gave classifiers a clue as to how specific or broad a range of LC numbers should be included in the profile. Without such information, many profiles would have been quite nebulous, for course descriptions themselves frequently failed to reflect the faculty member's actual research interests and areas of specialization.

    The profile constructed for one subject will illustrate the indexing technique of classifying courses and the difference in classed numbers developed for courses, publications and current research interests. It also reveals the difficulty of predicting from the catalog description the actual course content which a professor covers in the classroom. When requesting his permission to publish the profile, the faculty member noted that the catalog course description did not reflect the topics covered during the semester. Not agreeing with the catalog description, he developed the course along the lines he considered more appropriate.

SAMPLE PROFILE

Course Work

"CEN 231. Introduction to Chemical Engineering I. (3)

Laws of conservation of mass energy. Introduction to use of analog and conversational mode digital computers. Application of continuity equation to transient and steady state process. Prerequisites: CEN 106, 116, and MAT 296."

TP 155-156, "Chemical Engineering"
QC 73, "Physics--Force and energy, conservation and dissipation"
TK 7888 & 7888.3, "Electronics--Analog and Digital Computers"
QA 76.4, "Analog Computers"
QA 76.5, "Digital Computers"
TA 345, "Engineering with electronic data processing"

"CEN 786. Chemical Engineering Kinetics. (3)

Homogeneous reactions: tubular and stirred reactions, axial and radial transport. Resident time distribution. Heterogeneous reactions-catalytic: rates, pores, transport, in fixed and fluid beds, non-catalytic creation and growth of new phases. Prerequisites: CEN 587, 651 and 671."

TP 155-156, "Chemical Engineering"
QC 175, "Kinetic Theory of Gases"
QC 175.3, "Kinetic Theory of Liquids"

Research Interests (from interview and vita sheet)

1. Demineralization of water

TD 466, "Removal of dissolved materials, water softening"
TD 478-480.7, "Saline water conversion"

Methodology

2. Crystal Growth Rate

> TA 418.9 C_7, "Materials of special composition and structure; crystalline solids"
> TP 156.C_7, "Chemical Engineering Crystallization"
> QD 548, "Chemistry, supersaturated solutions, crystallizations"
> QD 921, "Crystal structure and growth. Liquid crystals"
> QD 951, "Chemical crystallography"

3. Chemical Engineering--mass transfer

> TP 155.7, "Chemical processes"
> TP 156.M_3, "Mass transfer"

Publications

> TD 433, "Water Purification"
> *QD 1, "Chemistry periodicals"
> *TP 1, "Chemical technology periodicals"
> *T 178, "Special research laboratories-- industrial research"

---

* "Hard" numbers or LC class numbers obtained from main entries in the SU Library's union catalog.

After the classification of courses, the second step in developing profiles was to classify the research interests and publications of the sample members. During the interviews, researchers were asked to provide the investigators with a copy of their list of publications, to describe their current research interests, and to comment on whether or not the list reflected their current research interests. The classification of research interests did not involve any unique problems. On the other hand, publication titles were frequently ambiguous or misleading to classify. For those publications acquired and processed by the university library system, specific LC subject numbers from the main entry card were included in the interest profile.

<u>Procedural Notes</u>. Classification numbers assigned by students were reviewed by two professional catalogers. Disagreements between the two were resolved in conference.

When an individual's profile was checked as complete, the individual's card was then edited to eliminate duplicate numbers, to arrange the LC number in sequential order, and to group into spans when necessary. The completed profile was recorded on the back of the subject's card and a duplicate copy made for subsequent use in the shelf list count of document dispersion patterns. The one hundred profiles are not included in order to conceal the identity of the respondents.

LIMITATIONS OF INTEREST PROFILES

Several factors could serve to limit the validity of an individual's interest profile. First, it has already been noted that course descriptions do not necessarily reflect the actual course content or the particular idiosyncracies and emphases of a faculty member who is teaching the course. Obviously, the emphasis a teacher places on the subject matter will affect the readings he assigns and his own relative information needs. Second, the subject teaching and research interests of faculty are not static. When faculty were asked during the interview if their list of publications and course load reflected current research interests, 59 percent of the SU and 22 percent of the OSU interviewees reported in the negative. Some academic departments require their faculty to rotate instruction of certain courses. The instructional load of others is almost exclusively related to advising doctoral students or supervising reading and research students whose selected topic may or may not coincide with the faculty member's primary interest.

A third possible limitation relates to the structure of hierarchical classification schemes such as the Library of Congress System or the Dewey Decimal System. It was sometimes impossible to select a number, or numbers, to represent adequately certain concepts. For example, the LC "H" schedule offers a span of numbers ranging from HF 5801 to 6181 for various subheadings under "Advertising." None of them, however, seems specifically suited to the economic and social aspects of advertising. Inclusion of the entire range or just specific numbers within the range would be tantamount to suggesting that a great deal of extraneous material is actually relevant to the individual's interest profile. On the other hand, the exclusion of a few or several numbers would undoubtedly eliminate potentially relevant materials. Furthermore, many LC schedules have not been formally revised and updated for years. For example, Class L,

Education, does not begin to reflect the educational scene today. For audio-visual media in education, the schedule has a span of LB 1043 to 1044.9. The terms "media" or "Instructional Technology" are non-existent in the index to Class L. Perhaps new numbers have been assigned to current topics, but profile classification, unlike book classification, does not permit a search of the LC Card Number Index to National Union Catalog.[13] If the subject headings catalog[14] does not list a number, there is little a classifier, constructing profiles, can do to provide one for many current subjects.

Such factors must be considered when constructing faculty interest profiles. Class numbers cannot be assigned mechanically in a vacuum. Rather, classifiers must take into account the restraints inherent in both the classification scheme employed and in the idiosyncracies of both the university environment and the individual faculty member. Therefore, the authors can testify once again that classification, whether of books, courses, or people, is indeed an art.

SHELF LIST COUNT OF DOCUMENT DISPERSION PATTERN

Following the completion of subject interest profiles, the class numbers representing each faculty member's interest profile were searched in the library shelf list. The locations of all titles assigned specific class numbers were recorded for each faculty member in order to determine the dispersion of potentially relevant documents. The document dispersion pattern was designed to yield the following information relative to each faculty member's subject profile: (1) total number of documents housed in the library system which match the specific class numbers of the interest profile, and (2) the dispersion and location of the documents relative to the individual's library use pattern.

Procedure. The instructions given to students counting library holdings and locations for each individual document dispersion pattern are in Appendix B-1. After a brief training session, the students took an edited interest profile card which identified all LC subject numbers for a given subject and the list of libraries used in rank order of their use. The following is a sample of an edited interest profile card for use in the shelf list count.

Figure 1: EDITED INTEREST PROFILE CARD
FOR STUDENT USE IN SHELF LIST COUNT

Subject code number: 048

QC 1
QC 173
QC 415
QC 447
QC 481-482
QC 721   Libraries used:
QC 757
QD 901   (1) Engineering
QD 921   (2) Physics
QD 931-941   (3) Chemistry
QD 945   (4) Carnegie
QH 201-219
T 1
TA 418.5
TJ 940
TN 1
TN 690

When the document dispersion pattern was completed for each individual, the number of titles was summed up for each class number and each library used. Then the percentage of total relevant holdings was calculated for each library containing materials of interest to the subject. By comparing the percent of materials included in the libraries used against the total dispersed throughout the system, the researchers established the respondent's document exposure index (DEI). In addition, all worksheets were checked against the edited interest profile on the original classed 5" x 8" card to be sure that all LC subject numbers and spans were included in the shelf list count. A sample document dispersion pattern worksheet is found in Appendix B-2.

Information Included in the Document Dispersion Pattern. From the document dispersion pattern, one can readily discern the total number of libraries which housed potentially relevant materials, the percent of those materials housed in each library, and whether or not the researcher used those libraries containing documents of interest to him. In other words, the pattern of dispersion should highlight how the choice of libraries would influence his potential for obtaining

Methodology

successfully the information he needs through the library system. As an example, the pattern presented in Table 6 shows that the subject's library use was concentrated on a library which housed a mere 17 percent of the documents of potential interest to him, although the second library contained 82 percent of the relevant materials. Note that a "non-substantial" or "ns" level was arbitrarily designated for library holdings equaling less than one percent of an individual's total relevant holdings.

Table 6. A SAMPLE DOCUMENT DISPERSION PATTERN OF ONE FACULTY MEMBER

Library	Percent holdings	Rank Lib. used	Rank of holdings
Maxwell	17	1	2
Carnegie	82		1
University College	ns		
Journalism	ns		
	99+		

Limitations of the Shelf List Count of Document Dispersion Patterns. In general, the limitations were attributed to organizational and procedural idiosyncracies inherent in every institution. Factors indigenous to the Syracuse University Library system are as follows:

1. Dewey numbers. April 18, 1962, was the last day books were classified in the Dewey Decimal System at Syracuse University. An initial attempt to reclassify all materials was abandoned several years ago and the shelf list is divided into two sections, one for the LC and one for the Dewey materials. Although most Dewey numbers are stored in an annex one mile away and brought to the main library for pickup within three to five hours after an individual requests them, many are scattered in various branch locations throughout the system. Because of time limitations which included a scheduled move of the library's processing center in early May, there was no attempt to classify the subjects' interests according to Dewey. Thus, a large array of potentially relevant materials in various locations were eliminated from the library processing center count.

2. The Social Work Library is not an official branch of the library system. Most materials there are on long-term charge-out from the main library, and the shelf list location notation would cite the latter rather than social work. In addition, the School of Social Work purchases materials that are processed by the library processing center staff but are not included in the university shelf list. Thus, data pertaining to the document dispersion pattern of users of the School of Social Work Library were distorted.

3. Subjects using slides, films, ERIC documents, maps, and information in formats not classified in LC and not included in the shelf list holdings also have an incomplete interest profile.

4. "K" Schedule Numbers. The law numbers do not reflect the university's holdings because, for several years, books in that class have been labeled with a "K" or "law" plus a Cutter number while awaiting the completion of the LC "K" schedule. One person in the sample, not a member of the Law School, which was eliminated from the original population, used that library exclusively. Although the majority of the law books are located in the Law Library, many departments purchase law titles each year which are housed in a branch billed for the document. Nonetheless, only a very small percentage of the law materials were fully classified in LC and eligible for inclusion in the shelf list count.

5. "R" Schedule Materials. The university has acquired relatively few medical materials since 1962 when it was agreed that Upstate Medical Center would collect such materials. Many disciplines in both the physical and social sciences--biology, psychology, social work--may rely heavily on such materials and "R" numbers appeared in several profiles. Yet, most of the material noted in the shelf list probably would be somewhat outdated for most purposes, thus encouraging respondents to use the Upstate Medical Center Library whose holdings do not appear in the Syracuse shelf list.

Another factor to bear in mind in evaluating an individual's document dispersion pattern is the total lack of qualitative evaluation of the classed titles included. For instance, what percentage of the documents with a specific LC number are obsolete except from a historical point of view? Is the majority of the material in a specific class number too elementary to warrant the faculty member's attention? How many titles really do fall within the respondent's interest

Methodology 27

area? For example, the few LC numbers available for documents dealing with electronic data processing necessitate the inclusion of a broad range of material within a specific designated number. An individual interested in the use of digital computers in chemical analysis would probably find only a few out of a few hundred titles classed in QA 76.5 relevant to his needs, and probably not the same titles as the individual interested in their use in solving specific engineering problems.

Despite the constraints associated with the technique employed, the investigators considered the profile methodology a valid means to compare faculty interests and library use patterns against the dispersion of relevant materials throughout the library system.

DISTANCE MEASUREMENTS

Basically, the distances between offices and various library branches were derived with a map measure, following the paths from door to door on an official scaled map of the university campus.

To compensate for physical and psychological barriers to library usage--climbing stairs or looking for a parking space when driving to distant branches--amounts were arbitrarily added to the door-to-door measurements as follows:

1. Twenty feet if subject could use an elevator in a building to move from floor to floor, regardless of how many floors he must ascend or descend.

2. Forty feet for each flight of stairs subject had to climb both in his office building and in the library building. For Carnegie, the main library, second floor usage was assumed or an additional 40 feet added. Nothing was added to door-to-door measurement for users of the Music Library which is located on the first floor of Carnegie.

3. Two hundred feet if subject had to use his car to go to the library and then find a parking space.

In cases where the respondent's office or library was located outside the limits covered by the university map, distances were measured by an automobile speedometer from the off-limits point to a point on the map and converted into the footage scale employed with the map measure. The map measure was then used to complete the measurement to the library used. Thus, the following was added to the map measurements:

1. University College
   (a) 264 feet between University College and the corner of Crouse Avenue and East Genesee Street.
   (b) 330 feet between University College and University Avenue and East Genesee Street.

2. Collendale and Colvin Street office buildings
   721 feet to distance measured from the rear driveway of the Women's Building and Comstock Avenue.

3. Skytop Office Building
   1188 feet from the Women's Building and Comstock Avenue.

SPECIAL EVALUATION MEASUREMENTS

The investigators developed two measurements to describe faculty members' attitudes toward the library system and their success in retrieving resources from the system. During the interview, respondents were asked to estimate what was their expectation that when they left the library, they would have the specific document they wanted in hand. The expectation rate, ER, is simply the rating on a scale from 0 to 10 which a person assigns as his chances of retrieving successfully a specified document on any one occasion. In a few cases, the subject specified several ERs to represent different types of materials--books and journals-- or for different branches in the system. The average ER was assigned arbitrarily as the ER in those instances.

The second measure, the document exposure index, DEI, is simply the percent of total holdings falling within an individual's subject interest profile which are housed in the libraries he uses. For example, a professor who uses the chemistry and physics libraries which house collectively 75 percent of the documents of interest to him has a DEI of 75 percent.

Summary. The study embodies a number of data collection techniques, each designed to fulfill specific requirements in the data collection process:

1. The personal interviews with the structured guides not only developed a great deal of data on library use, information sources and attitudes toward delivery service, but also allowed investigators to probe for reasons underlying specific attitudes.

2. The expectation rate index, one of the new measurements developed by the investigators, indicated users' evaluation of the library system's effectiveness in meeting their informational needs.

3. The construction of subject interest profiles enabled investigators to "quantify" with LC subject numbers each Syracuse University sample member's teaching and research interests.

4. The development of document dispersion patterns for each faculty member made it possible to relate the individual's interests to his library usage and the location of relevant documents in the library system.

5. The document exposure index evaluated faculty members' utilization of the potentially relevant informational resources of the library system.

6. Finally, the distance measurements were necessary to determine what effect distance had on an individual's library usage compared with the location of relevant documents in the library system.

The six data collection techniques were well meshed to provide a multifaceted view of an individual's library use and attitudes toward the library system and its services. Furthermore, the methodologies combined to reveal the impact of library organizational structure on user accessibility of library resources.

Notes

11. Dougherty, R. M., "The evaluation of the document delivery service at the University of Colorado." College and Research Libraries, Vol. 34, No. 1 (January, 1973), pp. 29-39.

12. McGrath, W. and Durand, N., "Classifying courses in the university catalog." College and Research Libraries, Vol. 30, No. 6 (November, 1969), pp. 533-9.

13. LC Card Number Index to the National Union Catalog, compiled and prepared by the staff of the Lisco Division. Cambridge, Mass., Data Operations, 1958- .

14. U.S. Library of Congress. Subject Cataloging Division. Subject Headings Used in the Dictionary Catalogs of the Library of Congress. Edited by Marguerite V. Quattlebaun. 7th ed., 1966.

Chapter III

RESULTS OF THE STUDY

LIBRARY USE AND DISPERSION OF MATERIALS

As stated earlier, the scattering of documents throughout a typical decentralized university library system could possibly be a deterrent to researchers' full utilization of library resources. An analysis displaying the dispersion of relevant documents for each individual in the SU sample is shown in Table 7. It shows the number of libraries in which materials relevant to the teaching and research interests of each individual are located, the number of libraries each subject claimed to have used, the document exposure index (DEI), and his expectation rate (ER). The underlined percents reflect the holdings in libraries the respondents used in the rank order of usage. For example, the biologist (069) who expressed an ER of 9.0 believed that he is able to locate 90 percent of the documents relevant to him in the only library he uses, a library which houses only 69 percent of the materials potentially relevant to him. Because he used only that library, his DEI was also 69. In contrast, the engineer (073) with an expressed ER of 7.0 should retrieve only nine percent of the potentially relevant materials in the library he uses first. Yet, his DEI was 98 percent because he was willing to search in three additional libraries.

The impact of decentralized collections can be illustrated by focusing on the library use and holdings for researchers in the College of Engineering. The data presented in Table 7 suggest that engineers are willing to use more libraries than some of their fellow researchers. Yet, it is equally apparent that many relevant resources were not coming under their scrutiny. Materials of interest to faculty from engineering were located in 8.2 libraries, whereas those interviewed used, on the average, 3.7 libraries (figures derived from data presented in Table 7). One might argue that the most relevant materials were located in the libraries they

(cont. p. 37)

Key to Table 7

1. Underlined numbers represent the libraries each individual uses.

2. Holdings are listed in the table in the order in which subjects used a library, e.g., number 123 had 70 percent of relevant materials in his first choice library, 8 percent in his second, etc.

3. Holdings are expressed in percent, i.e., 70 = percent of potentially relevant documents housed in subject 123's first used library.

4. ns = non-substantial holdings--less than one percent of total relevant holdings.

5. DEI, the document exposure index, or percent of total potentially relevant holdings housed in the libraries the subject uses.

6. ER, the expectation rate, is the rating on a scale from 0 to 10 which a person assigns as his chances of successfully retrieving a specified document on any one occasion.

Results of the Study 33

SUMMARY OF LIBRARY USE, DOCUMENT DISPERSION PATTERNS, DEI AND ER FOR EACH SU SAMPLE MEMBER

Department & Code		1st	2nd	3rd	4th	5th	6th	7th	8th	9th	10th	11th	12th	Total Lib. Holding Docs.	Total Lib. Used	Total Holdings of First Lib.	DEI	ER
Group I – Sciences																		
Air Force	061	65	23	6	5									4	1	65	65	8.0
Biology	069	69	17	5	4	2	2							6	1	69	69	9.0
	123	70	8	19	2	1	ns	ns						7	3	70	97	7.0
Chemistry	020	87	4	4	3	2	ns	ns						7	1	87	87	10.0
	034	37	37	2	1	12	11	ns						7	4	37	77	7.5
	044	80	2	12	4	2	ns	ns						7	2	80	82	9.0
	051	54	21	19	4	2	1	ns	ns	ns	ns			10	3	54	94	10.0
Engineering	017	60	21	16	1	1	1							6	2	60	81	3.5
	023	38	27	12	11	9	3	ns	ns	ns	ns			10	6	38	100	5.0
	024	56	7	19	8	3	3	1	1	1	ns			10	2	56	63	6.0
	039	46	15	28	6	3	1	ns	ns					8	2	46	61	7.0
	048	24	47	16	5	6	2	ns	ns					8	4	24	92	8.0
	070	38	53	1	ns	7	1							6	5	38	99	7.0
	073	9	2	24	2	1	ns	ns	ns					8	4	9	98	7.0
	075	75	63	11	0	6	2	2	1	ns				8	5	75	94	6.5
	094	58	2	10	11	1	1	1	ns	ns	ns			10	3	58	86	6.0
Human Development	037	11	43	23	23	ns	ns	ns						6	3	11	77	8.0
Mathematics	018	86	9	2	2	ns	ns	ns						7	1	86	86	9.0
Physics	122	62	6	17	9	4	2	ns						7	2	62	68	9.5
Psychology	013	49	19	16	9	4	1	ns	ns	ns	ns	ns		12	1	49	49	none
	025	96	2	1	ns	ns	ns	ns	ns					9	1	96	96	7.0
	026	52	34	7	2	2	1	1	ns	ns				9	1	52	52	0.0
	060	80	7	3	2	2	2	1	1	1	1	ns		11	1	80	80	4.0
Science Teaching	062	60	33	2	2	1	1	ns	ns	ns	ns	ns	ns	12	1	60	60	6.0

Table 7 (continued)

Department & Code		1st	2nd	3rd	4th	5th	6th	7th	8th	9th	10th	11th	12th	Total Lib. Holding Docs.	Total Lib. Used	% Holdings of First Lib.	DEI	ER
Group II - Social Sciences																		
Air Force	009	70	10	9	8	2	1	ns	ns					8	0	0	0	0.0
Anthropology	084	88	ns	7	2	1	1	ns	ns	ns	ns			10	2	88	88	5.0
	092	91	2	5	1	1	ns							6	3	91	98	5.0
	119	96	1	1	1	ns	ns	ns	ns	ns				9	1	96	96	5.0
Army, ROTC	121	0	70	10	10	8	1	ns	ns					7	1	0	0	7.0
Economics	050	22	70	ns	1	3	1	1	1	ns	ns			10	4	22	93	6.0
	090	71	25	2	1	1	ns	1	ns	ns				9	2	71	96	5.0
	115	85	5	ns	6	1	1	1	ns	ns	ns			10	4	85	96	1.0
Education	010	87	5	4	2	1	ns	ns	ns					8	0	0	0	none
	021	89	4	3	2	1	1	ns	ns					8	1	89	89	3.5
	038	97	1	1	ns	ns	ns	ns						7	1	97	97	8.0
	040	10	56	13	8	6	3	1	1	1	ns	ns		11	1	10	10	8.0
	054	95	2	2	ns	ns	ns	ns	ns	ns				9	1	95	95	5.5
	057	95	4	ns	ns	ns	ns	ns	ns					8	1	95	95	none
	058	99	ns	ns	ns									4	1	99	99	6.0
Geography	029	14	72	7	2	2	1	1	ns	ns	ns	ns	ns	12	3	14	93	7.5
	071	20	74	2	4	ns	ns	ns	ns					8	4	20	100	2.5
	080	88	4	2	2	1	1	1	ns	ns				9	2	88	92	6.0
History	008	85	5	3	1	2	2	1	ns					8	5	85	96	5.0
	045	75	21	2	1	ns								5	2	75	96	5.0
	072	90	7	1	1	ns	ns	ns	ns	ns	ns			10	2	90	97	3.0
	097	79	8	4	ns	4	3	1	1					8	4	79	91	4.0
	110	72	14	6	4	2	1	ns	ns					8	2	72	86	8.0
	116	96	1	2	ns	ns	ns							5	2	96	97	7.5
	118	97	ns	2	1	ns	ns	ns						7	3	97	99	3.0

Results of the Study 35

Table 7 (continued)

Department & Code		1st	2nd	3rd	4th	5th	6th	7th	8th	9th	10th	11th	12th	Total Lib. Holding Docs.	Total Lib. First Used	% Holdings of Lib.	DEI	ER
Human Development	053	83	7	7	2	1								5	2	83	90	5.0
	091	94	2	1	1	1								10	2	94	96	9.0
	111	5	86	4	2	1	ns	ns	ns	ns	ns			9	2	5	91	7.5
Management	014	68	6	16	6	2	1	ns	ns	ns	ns			11	4	68	96	5.0
	064	72	1	1	19	4	2	ns	ns	ns	ns	ns		11	3	72	74	5.0
	088	85	8	3	2	1	ns	ns	ns					8	0	0	0	1.0
	113	97	0	ns	2	ns	ns							5	3	97	97	6.5
	114	83	6	4	4	2	ns	ns		ns				10	1	83	83	5.0
Political Science	056	40	55	2	2	1	ns	ns	1	1				8	3	40	97	4.0
	089	59	27	4	3	1	1	1	1		ns	ns	ns	12	2	59	86	6.0
	105	17	82	ns	ns									4	1	17	17	0.0
Public Communications	001	15	79	3	2	1	ns	ns	ns	ns				9	2	15	94	9.0
	085	0	87	5	4	3	1	ns	ns	ns				8	2	0	87	2.0
Social Work	003	8	88	2	2	ns	ns	ns	ns	ns				9	3	8	98	6.0
	007	4	91	ns	1	1	1	1	1	ns	ns	ns		11	3	4	95	7.0
	035	13	3	75	6	2	1	ns	ns	ns				9	2	13	16	9.0
	059	20	ns	69	6	1	1	1	1	ns	ns			10	3	20	89	5.0
	093	21	74	3	2	ns	1	ns	ns	ns				5	2	21	95	7.5
	098	7	78	9	3	1	1	4	1	ns				9	3	7	94	8.0
Sociology	106	62	1	14	2	10	5	4	1	ns	ns	ns	ns	12	4	62	79	1.0
Group III - Humanities																		
Architecture	012	54	ns	39	4	1	1	ns	ns					8	3	54	93	8.0
	032	32	35	26	1	ns	0	4	1	ns	ns			9	6	32	94	6.0
	096	52	11	37	1									3	2	52	63	4.5
English	002	96	3	1	ns	ns	ns	ns						7	1	96	96	5.0
	005	78	19	1	ns	ns	ns	ns						7	0	0	0	5.0

Table 7 (continued)

Department & Code		1st	2nd	3rd	4th	5th	6th	7th	8th	9th	10th	11th	12th	Total Lib. Holding Docs.	Total Lib. Used	% Holdings of First Lib.	DEI	ER
Fine Arts	022	97	1	1	ns	ns								5	1	97	97	2.0
	027	99	ns	ns	ns									4	1	99	99	5.0
	011	100	ns	ns	ns									4	2	100	100	5.5
	015	96	3	1										3	2	96	99	7.0
German	049	92	8	ns	ns									4	1	92	92	5.0
Human Development	081	59	31	8	1	1								5	1	59	59	6.5
	082	90	2	ns										3	1	90	90	6.5
Library Science	099	96	1	1	1	1	ns	ns	ns	ns				9	2	96	97	5.0
Philosophy	074	98	1	ns	ns	ns	ns	ns	ns	ns				5	2	98	99	7.0
	086	94	4	1	1	ns	ns	ns	ns	ns				9	1	94	94	8.5
Religion	042	98	ns	1	1	1								4	2	98	98	3.5
	112	85	2	ns	ns	13	ns							7	4	85	87	5.5
Romance Languages	095	99	ns	ns	ns									4	1	99	99	5.0
Visual & Performing Arts	016	99	1	ns										3	2	99	100	8.0
	019	100	ns											2	1	100	100	7.5
	030	97	3											2	1	97	97	8.0
	033	95	5											2	1	95	95	5.0
	036	2	95	ns	3									4	3	2	97	2.0
	063	86	2	3	2	2	1	1	1	1	ns			10	2	86	88	2.0
	067	100												1	1	100	100	5.0
	079	97	3											2	1	97	97	5.0
	087	66	31	3										3	2	66	97	8.0
	103	71	10	15	2	1	1	ns						7	3	71	96	5.0
	104	98	2	ns		1	1	ns						3	2	98	100	5.0
	107	89	ns	8	1	1	ns	ns						7	2	89	89	7.5
	120	99	1	ns										3	2	99	100	9.0

used. On the other hand, one could argue equally cogently that the most important materials were housed in the libraries they did not use. Which is true is not known; there is probably some truth to both views.

Table 8. SUMMARY OF GROUP RANGES AND MEANS OF LIBRARY USE, HOLDINGS AND EXPECTATION RATE

Group	n	No. Lib. Housing Docs.	No. Lib. Used	Exposure Index 1st Lib.	DEI	ER
Group means						
Sciences	24	8.2	2.5	57	80	7.0
Social Sciences	45	8.4	2.2	54	79	5.0
Humanities	31	4.8	1.7	82	91	5.9
Group ranges						
Sciences	24	4-12	1-6	9-96	49-100	0-10
Social Sciences	45	4-13	0-5	0-99	0-100	0-9
Humanities	31	1-10	0-6	0-100	0-100	2-9

Table 8 summarizes the ranges and means of libraries used and holdings for the three groups: sciences, social sciences and humanities. For all three groups, the mean number of libraries that researchers frequented is far below the number of libraries housing potentially relevant materials. It should be noted that the investigators had neither the time nor the resources to verify whether or not subjects actually used the libraries they claimed to use. A sampling of circulation records was suggested, but it is well known how imperfect circulation is as a measure of use. Because actual use was not verified, and respondents were asked to cite all libraries they had used at one time or another, the results probably overstate use of the library system. In fact, many respondents did use terms like "rarely" or "seldom" when listing second, third, etc. libraries used. In other words, the DEI's for many users are much too high.

A variety of interpretations may be drawn from the data displayed in Tables 7 and 8. Obviously, the materials for most users are dispersed throughout many libraries and the dispersion is most prominent among the sciences. Even for the humanities, where the majority of materials are most

(cont. p. 42)

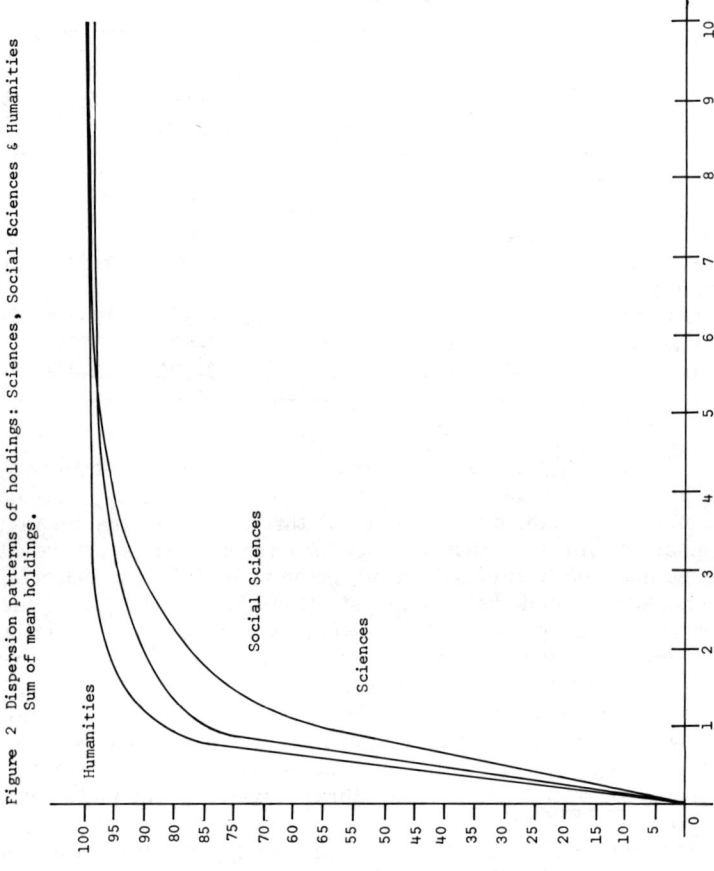

Figure 2 Dispersion patterns of holdings: Sciences, Social Sciences & Humanities Sum of mean holdings.

Results of the Study   39

1. Sciences	2. Social Sciences	3. Humanities
1 – 61.9	1 – 81.2	1 – 87.4
2 – 82.1	2 – 91.6	2 – 96.4
3 – 91.3	3 – 95.2	3 – 98.9
4 – 95.8	4 – 97.4	4 – 99.3
5 – 97.8	5 – 98.5	5 – 99.6
6 – 99.6	6 – 99.0	6 – 99.7
7 – 99.8	7 – 99.2	7 – 99.73
8 – 99.9	8 – 99.3	8 – 99.76
9 – 99.94	9 – 99.4	9 – 99.79
10 – 100	10 – 99.7	10 – 100

x = libraries with revelant holdings: 1st, 2nd, 3rd,....10th
y = per cent of relevant holdings

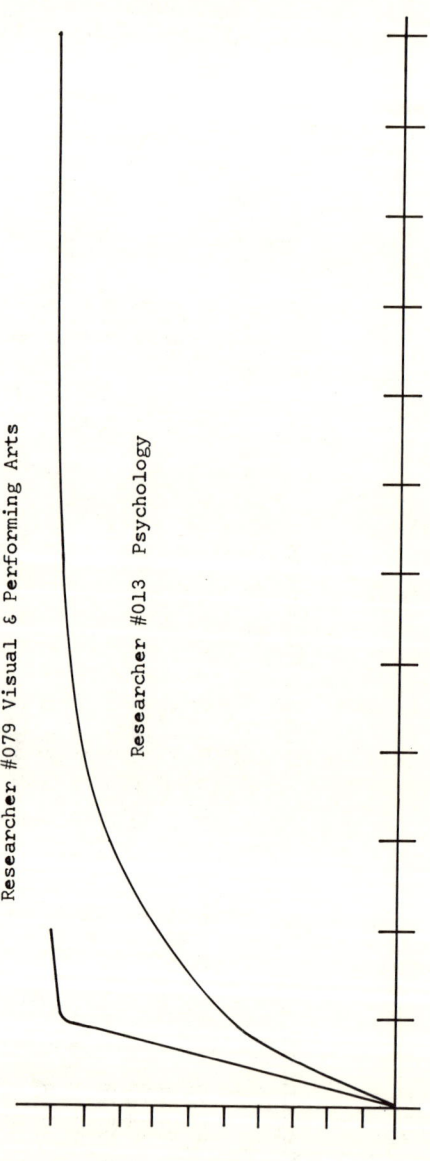

Figure 3. Contrast of dispersion of holdings for two researchers

Results of the Study

#013 - Psychology

1st lib	- 49%
2nd	- 68
3rd	- 84
4th	- 93
5th	- 97
6th	- 98
7th	- 98.4
8th	- 98.8
9th	- 99.2
10th	- 99.5
11th	- 98.8
12th	- 100

#079 Visual & Performing Arts

1st lib	- 97%
2nd	100

x - Libraries with relevant holdings
    1st, 2nd ... 12th

y - per cent of relevant holdings

See Appendix pg.   for figure data.

likely to be found either in the central library or in the storage stacks, there are materials of potential relevance scattered throughout the system. The effect of the scattering of materials for the humanities, social sciences and sciences is shown in Figure 2. The cumulative curves graphically depict the concentration of materials for the humanities as compared to the greater scattering for the social sciences and the sciences.

To further illustrate the influence of library organization on the user's access to information, Figure 3 depicts the contrast for two individuals: one from visual and performing arts whose materials were concentrated in two library locations; the other from psychology whose materials were dispersed throughout twelve physical locations.

Table 9. COMPARISON OF PERCENT OF HOLDINGS WITH RANK OF LIBRARY USED

Percent Holdings	Rank of Libraries Used					
	1st	2nd	3rd	4th	5th	6th
0-ns	1	9*	7	4	2	1
1-10	6	26*	14	10	5	1
11-20	7	4	8	1		
21-30	3	6	2	1		
31-40	5	3	1			
41-50	2	1	1			
51-60	9	3				
61-70	7	2		1		
71-80	8	6				
81-90	13	2	2			
91-100	29	3				
Other library	6	6	5	1		
No library	4					
Total	100	71	40	18	7	2

* The percent of holdings between 0-10% for second ranked libraries is of little significance because many in this category are a result of the twenty-nine instances when the first ranked library held 91-100% of the relevant materials.

Another measure of the effect of dispersed holdings was revealed by an analysis of the percent of holdings in libraries compared to the relative ranking of libraries used (Table 9). Although the first-choice library of many researchers (42%) contained 80 to 100 percent of their potentially relevant documents, the first-choice library of others was not the library with the most extensive holdings. Twenty-four percent of the SU faculty's first-choice libraries housed 50 percent or less of the materials of potential interest to them.

DISPERSION OF HOLDINGS AND USERS' EXPECTATION RATE

The investigators were extremely interested in exploring the relationship between the expectation rates of users and the holdings of the libraries they used. In other words, would a user's expectation rate increase as the holdings of the libraries he used became more comprehensive, thus increasing the probability of his locating the needed materials? Even a casual visual inspection of the expectation rates as shown in Table 7 suggests that there is little or no relationship between the DEIs of either the first or all of the libraries combined and an individual's ER. The absence of any statistically significant relationship was verified by using the step-wise regression procedure where the purpose of the analysis was to identify relationships between holdings and ERs of all subjects and the ERs of individuals within each group--sciences, social sciences and humanities.* The test produced no significant correlations. Thus, in the SU test environment, the depth of holdings was not a predictor of a person's expectation rate.

---

*Expectation rate as predicted by rank of holdings of the library used first and rank of distance of library used first was subjected to a multiple regression analysis using the step-wise regression procedure with ten dummy variables representing controls for comparing the effects of ten departmental libraries with the main library. The description of the method used can be found in: Draper, N. R. and H. Smith, Applied Regression Analysis. New York: Wiley, 1966. The computer program used to perform the analysis was the BMDO2R step-wise regression computer program: Dixon, W. J., BMD Biomedical Computer Programs. Berkeley: University of California Press, 1970. (Univ. of California Publications in Automatic Computation, No. 2).

The small sample size for some of the libraries may have masked the relationship between holdings and ERs but the lack of any significant correlation suggested that other variables are of greater importance to a user's satisfaction. The notion is supported by the comments gathered during the interviews which suggested that the more significant variables were possibly the availability of parking facilities, the geographic layout of the campus, the number of branches and their location. Other factors contributing to user satisfaction were service orientation of the library staff and the environmental conditions in the particular library, i.e., was it an attractive, comfortable place to work? Typical was the faculty member who observed about the main library, "What a dismal, horrible place. I can't work there. I don't feel that I can ask my students to spend time there." [Note that a move to the new building was scheduled for the summer of 1972.] Several others, in commenting on their preference for a nearby medical library, noted how easy it was to use the journals and how pleasant it was to work there.

LIBRARY USE AND DISTANCE

While there seemed to be little relationship between user expectation rate and holdings, the distance of a researcher's office from the libraries he used seemed to be a more positive predictor. As shown in Table 10, 16 percent of the subjects interviewed frequented libraries which were closest to their offices even though the library housed 50 percent or less of the materials of potential relevance to them. At the other extreme, 25 percent of the subjects used libraries with holdings equal to or greater than 80 percent even though these libraries were not closest to them. This superficial analysis thus supports the traditional view that richness of resources will draw some users from longer distances. These results are also congruent with the data collected by Berelson and his colleagues during the Public Library Inquiry conducted more than a generation ago.[15]

A chi square compared the distance to libraries of less than 12,500 feet and more than 12,500 feet with libraries used and not used. The analysis produced a highly significant chi square value (Table 11).

Another series of chi square analyses testing for differences between distance and use and non-use were run for the following relatively short distance categories: 0-1250 feet

Results of the Study 45

Table 10. COMPARISON OF HOLDINGS AND DISTANCE OF LIBRARIES USED FIRST

Percent Holdings	Distance of library used first	
	Closest	Not Closest
0-10	5	2
11-20	6	1
21-30	1	1
31-40	2	3
41-50	2	1
51-60	4	5
61-70	1	6
71-80	2	6
81-90	3	10
91-100	14	15
	40	50
OTHER LIBRARY	6	
NO LIBRARY	4	

Table 11. CHI SQUARE: DISTANCE OF LIBRARIES USED AND NOT USED (less than 12,500 feet and more than 12,500 feet)

Distance	Libraries Used	Libraries Not Used	Totals
12,500' or less	208	207	415
more than 12,500'	7	68	75
	215	275	490

magnitude of effect, $c = .27$ $x^2 = 41.27$ (significant at $.05\ x^2_{1df} = 3.84$).

to 1275-2500 feet; 1275-2500 feet to 2525-3750 feet; 2525-3750 feet to 3775-5000 feet.* None of the tests produced

---

*Note again that door-to-door distances from researchers' offices and the libraries they used were increased varying amounts to compensate for number of flights of stairs climbed, the inconvenience of seeking parking space, etc. See discussion under distance in Chapter II.

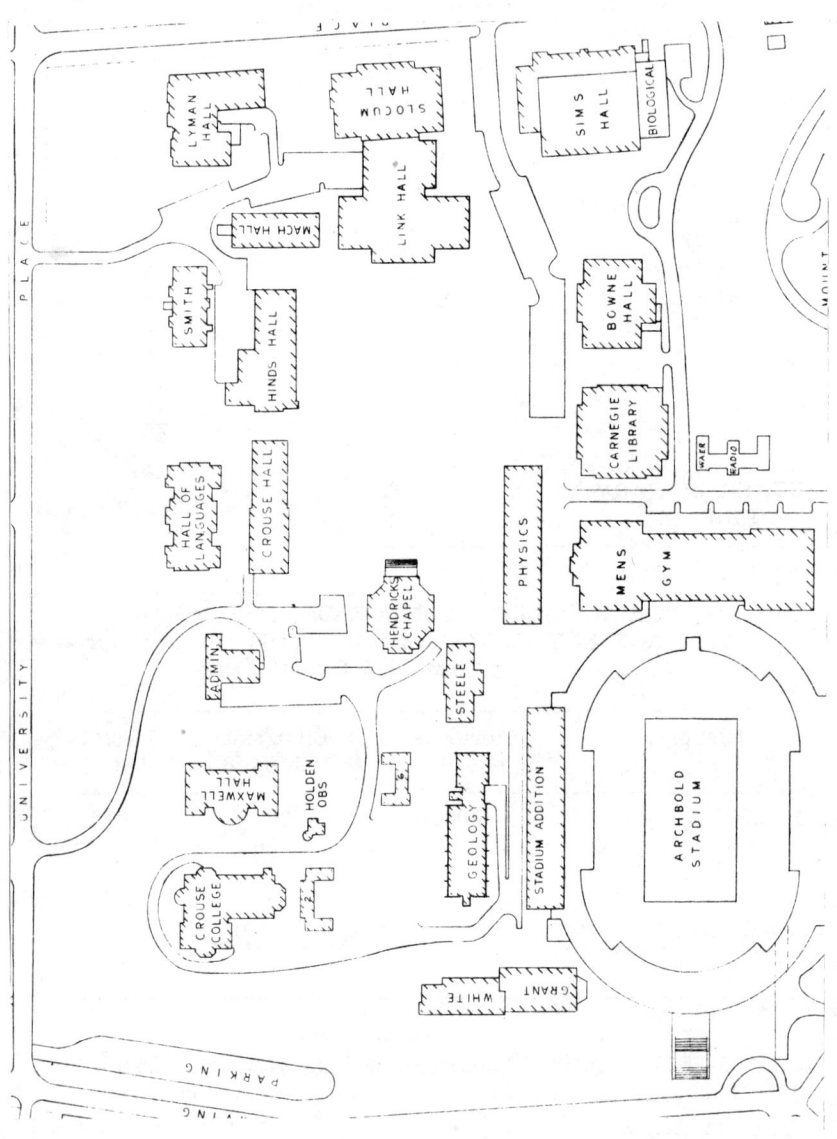

Figure 4. Syracuse University (section)

Results of the Study

significant chi square values. The findings of these tests may in part reflect the peculiarities of the SU campus. Most of the offices and libraries involved are located in the central quad area. Most of the libraries are within easy walking distance. (The central quad area is outlined in Figure 4.)

A step-wise multiple regression analysis compared expectation rate with rank of holdings of first choice library and the distance from an individual's office to his first choice library. It showed no correlation between ER and rank of holdings, and a positive though weak correlation of $r = .39$ between ER and distance of library. In both tests, distance did account for some of the observed variations. The correlation partially supported the contention stated earlier that other factors such as parking facilities, organization and accessibility of journals, bright reading areas, and service attitudes of the librarian may also influence choice of library used by researchers.

EXPECTATION RATINGS OF LIBRARY USERS

At both Syracuse and Ohio State, each interviewee was asked to estimate the likelihood that, when he went to the library to locate a specific item, he would have the item in hand when he left the library. Subjects were asked to rate their expectation on a scale from 0-10, with five interpreted to mean that he expected to find the item one-half of the time, and ten all of the time. (See questionnaires, Appendices A-2, D-1, and E-1.) The question was designed to sample an individual's feelings toward the library's effectiveness in meeting his information needs. The expectation rate is a subjective measure and should not be considered an actual measure of the library's ability to provide relevant materials.

<u>Expectation Rates of Syracuse University Faculty</u>. The overall mean expectation rate of users of a library in an environment without document delivery service was 5.76 (Appendix A-3). Obviously, many library users did not express optimism over their chances of retrieving specific documents. In fact, forty-two percent of the SU sample believed that they would find one-half or less of the documents sought (See Table 13). This finding was singularly disturbing for several reasons. First, the value, as expected, was entirely emotional; second, the library probably could have performed better if users had been instructed on how to locate docu-

ments; and third, as will be discussed later, no statistical relationship between ER and extensiveness of holdings was observed. In other words, factors other than library holdings play a powerful role in influencing users' expectation.

Further scrutiny revealed several corollary attitudes. SU faculty who used branch libraries exhibited a much higher expectation rate than those who used the central library. The mean expectation rate varied with the proximity of the offices to the first choice library. The mean expectation rates were expressed as follows: $\overline{X}ER = 7.39$ for respondents with access to a branch located in the same building as their office; $\overline{X}ER = 6.58$ for a branch located in a different building; and $\overline{X}ER = 4.88$ for the central library. The disparity of mean ERs between branch and central library was even more striking when all users whose first-used library was a branch were compared with users whose first-used library was the central facility. In the analysis, the mean expectation rate of those who used branches was 7.00, as compared to 5.10 for the central library (Table 12). Understandably, subjects exhibited progressively lower expectation rates as the library they used became more remote to them.

Table 12. SU EXPECTATION RATES AND FIRST USED LIBRARY: CENTRAL vs BRANCH

Expectation Rate	First Used Library	
	Central	Branch
0-1.0	2	1
1.1-2.0	2	
2.1-3.0	2	
3.1-4.0	4	1
4.1-5.0	15	7
5.1-6.0	5	7
6.1-7.0	3	10
7.1-8.0	5	13
8.1-9.0	1	7
9.1-10.0	0	3
No ER	2	
Totals*	41	49
MEAN ER	5.10	7.00

*Ten individuals named a non-university system library as their first choice library.

Results of the Study

Although generalizations about the attitudes expressed in the test environment may not be made for researchers on other campuses, one interpretation of far-reaching significance to librarians is that many users apparently are willing to forego accessibility to potentially relevant materials in favor of convenience of access. The differential in expectation rates plus the comments offered during the interviews made this interpretation, in the opinion of the investigators, unavoidable. On face value, it would appear that some users are willing to forego comprehensiveness for ease of use. Realistically, the interpretation, taken at face value, is probably overly simplistic. There are other equally plausible explanations. For example, a specialized branch library may be easier to maintain, offer a more hospitable environment and have an academically better qualified librarian who is closer to his/her group of users. In the opinion of the researchers, such variables did indeed contribute to more positive branch user attitudes. Nonetheless, the essential conclusion should not be ignored.

COMPARISON OF SU AND OSU FACULTY EXPECTATION RATES

One principal objective of the investigation was to compare the expectation rates of faculty users in two environments: one in which a document delivery system was available and one in which it was not. Fifty-nine known users of the Ohio State University Library delivery system were interviewed during the week of May 8-12. The results of the interviews, which were in striking contrast to the SU sample of users, are shown in Table 13. Although it is realized that the two samples are not comparable statistically speaking, the expectation rates expressed by OSU subjects prior to the introduction of the document delivery system were about as low as those expressed by SU faculty. OSU respondents expressed an average pre-delivery ER of 5.89 as compared to the test environment's ER of 5.76.

It is noteworthy that 35 (59 percent) of the 59 OSU subjects claimed to have a different ER before the introduction of the delivery service, and their mean change in ER was +2.56 with the inception of delivery services. Only four of the respondents had a lower ER post-delivery than pre-delivery, and each of them stated that they felt their lower ER was a result of greater demand on the resources from more borrowers because of the delivery service (Table 14).

It is possible that a halo effect may have biased the results, in that some subjects tried very hard to underscore how much they liked the service. Yet, the range in the change of the ERs, from -2 to +7, suggests that the halo effect was not very substantial. One can debate the validity of any comparisons, but it is the opinion of the investigators that it would be professionally imprudent to ignore unmistakable user preferences.

Table 13. FREQUENCY DISTRIBUTION OF EXPECTATION RATES: COMPARISON BETWEEN SU AND OSU (percent of sample)

Expectation Rate	SU	OSU prior to delivery	OSU with delivery
0-1.0	6	0	0
1.1-2.0	3	0	0
2.1-3.0	3	14	2
3.1-4.0	6	3	2
4.1-5.0	24	22	3
5.1-6.0	12	12	7
6.1-7.0	13	18	30
7.1-8.0	19	22	29
8.1-9.0	8	7	14
9.1-10.0	3	2	13
No ER	3		
	100	100	100

The mean expectation rate of the users interviewed on the OSU campus after the delivery service had been operating for a year was 7.62. An analysis of variance between the OSU users and the test environment produced significant results (although admittedly the two samples are not statistically comparable) in the observed expectation rates of the two samples. Another indication of the difference between the two attitudes was shown in a comparison of the ER ranges for the two groups of subjects. The SU expectation rates ranged from 0 to 10 with a bimodal distribution which peaked at five and eight, whereas the ERs of OSU users of the delivery service were distributed much more narrowly with a single mode observed at the 7.0 level. The ERs of OSU non-users, however, were also arrayed in a bimodal distribution which peaked at five and eight (Figure 5).

Results of the Study

Table 14. CHANGE IN EXPECTATION RATE OF OSU FACULTY AFTER INTRODUCTION OF DELIVERY SERVICE

Change	f	%
+7	1	3
+6	2	6
+5	3	8
+4	4	11
+3	6	17
+2.5	1	3
+2	8	23
+1.5	3	8
+1	3	8
-0.5	1	3
-1	2	6
-2	1	3

Mean Change = +2.56

In the current study, the influence of recency of library experience on attitudes was underscored. When SU subjects were asked whether or not they were satisfied or dissatisfied the last time they tried to locate an item in the library, those who stated that they were satisfied, as a group, quoted a mean expectation rate of 7.0, while those who noted dissatisfaction expressed the significantly lower mean expectation rate of 4.3. A three-way analysis of variance produced a statistically significant difference at the .05 level. A similar relationship was revealed in the sampling among the subjects interviewed in the environment in which the document delivery service was offered. Those who were satisfied with their last use of the library system expressed a mean ER of 7.82, while those who were dissatisfied had a mean ER of 6.12. Apparently, satisfaction with a recent library visit breeds a higher expectation of success in future encounters and a more positive attitude toward the library. One reasonable interpretation is that a new library service could possibly create an entirely different attitudinal climate toward the library on a campus.

In summary, the Syracuse University subjects' expectations of retrieving desired documents on their own was similar to the Ohio State University subjects' expectations prior to the introduction of a delivery service; of course, it is not known if the ERs of SU faculty would also increase if a docu-

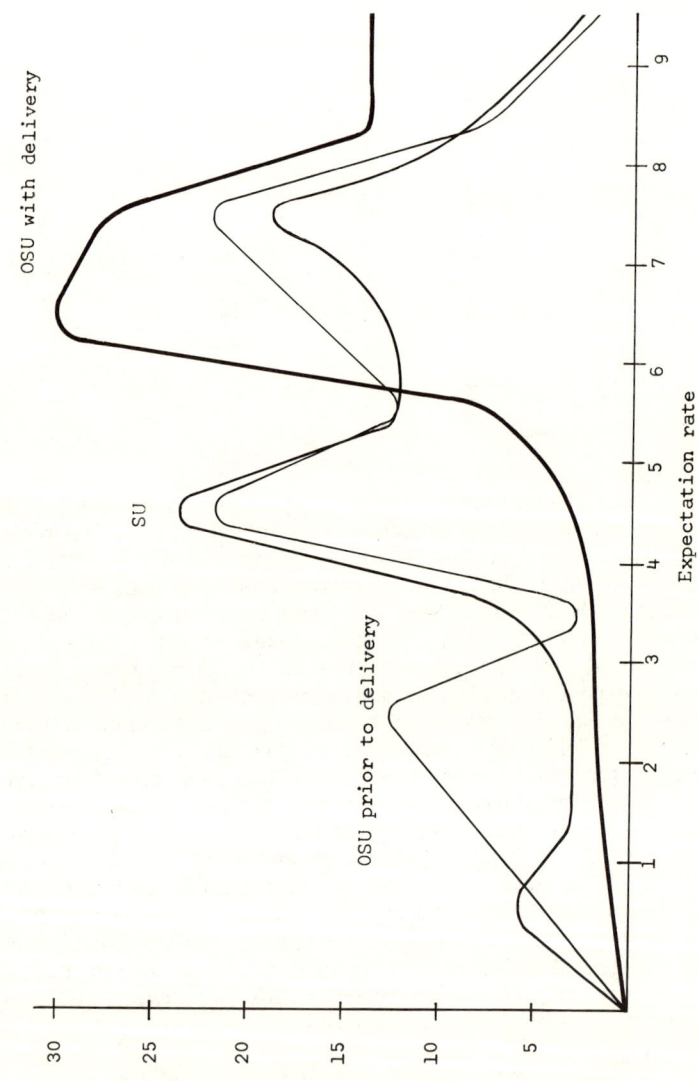

Figure 5 – Comparison of expectation rates. SU faculty with OSU faculty pre- and post delivery

Results of the Study 53

Er	SU	OSU with delivery	OSU prior to delivery
	%	%	%
0 - 1	6	-	-
1.1 - 2	3	2	14
2.1 - 3	3	2	3
3.1 - 4	6	3	22
4.1 - 5	24	7	12
5.1 - 6	12	30	18
6.1 - 7	13	28	22
7.1 - 8	19	14	7
8.1 - 9	8	14	2
9.1 - 10	3		

x - expectatopm rate, 0 - 10
y - per cent of respondents

ment delivery service were introduced at SU. As noted earlier, the mean ER for SU respondents was 5.76; for the OSU respondents prior to delivery, the mean ER was recollected to be 5.89. In contrast, the mean ER for OSU respondents after the delivery service was introduced increased to 7.62. Although many similarities in patterns were observed on the two campuses, including the similarity in the pre-document delivery ERs, again, we would be exceeding the limits of the data to conclude unequivocally that the delivery service alone produced the rise on OSU faculty ERs. An individual who was successful in obtaining materials on his last visit to the library tended to harbor more positive feelings toward the library than an individual who was unsuccessful on his last use of the library system. Although it may be important for librarians to understand why a search proved to be unsuccessful--that is, a document was charged out, was in another branch and not convenient to the user, or the user just did not know where to look for it--the reasons may well be immaterial to the user. Because he did not locate what he wanted and presumably needed, the library, in his eyes, had failed. The data do seem to suggest, however, that users who have access to materials through a delivery system are more satisfied with the library's performance.

EVALUATION OF THE DOCUMENT DELIVERY SERVICE

One objective of the study was to compare the attitudes of faculty in contrasting environments toward the same innovative service. The investigators' goal was to gain insights as to whether researchers reacted similarly before and after they had been exposed to an innovative service. If an attitudinal change was detectable, such evidence would support the hypothesis that the process of innovation diffusion in libraries is similar to patterns observed in other disciplines.

<u>Accessibility of Materials in a Document Delivery Environment</u>. OSU subjects were asked if the availability of a document delivery service had increased accessibility of library materials. The responses were extremely positive. Sixty-eight percent of the 59 subjects replied "Yes." Even the 32 percent who replied "No" offered positive explanations. For example, one person who stated "No" went on to explain that he still examined the same number of books but the delivery service made the process easier for him and reduced the frustrations associated with locating materials. Another

Results of the Study   55

person noted that the time-frame for inspection had been reduced. Still another advised that although he did not feel that he was inspecting more books, he did feel that the service had reduced the amount of time he was required to spend in the library.

Overall, users of the delivery system reported that they examined more items. Some volunteered that they were now examining as much as two or three times as many books as they had formerly scanned. When queried as to why, the responses usually fell into one or more of the following categories: the collections of the library were now more accessible, the library was easier to use, or it was more convenient to use. Several OSU respondents admitted that using the library formerly had been just too difficult for them. The time required to take a bus or find a parking spot in order to visit the branches in which materials of interest to them were located was simply not worth the effort. Now that materials were delivered to them, more books were examined than would ever have been examined a year or two ago. The claim was supported by the fact that circulation has increased by 31 percent since the introduction of the online circulation system and the document delivery system.[16]

Value of Delivery Service to OSU Faculty. Much of the data collected at OSU substantiated the value of the delivery service to its users. As Table 15 shows, 65 percent of the respondents stated that they requested materials via the delivery service more often than once per month. Twenty percent of them requested services more than once per week. Although only monographs were available through the service at the time the investigators were on campus, 37 percent of those interviewed claimed that the delivery service fulfilled over 50 percent of their library needs (Table 15). Furthermore, in answer to another question, 93 percent gave the delivery service a good or excellent rating.

When asked if their pattern of library use had changed since the introduction of the service, 86 percent of the 59 respondents answered in the affirmative. Sixty-one percent stated that they now used more library resources. In noting what a time-saver the service was, one respondent said he appreciated the elimination of his personal search time through the stacks and branches for desired documents. On the other hand, another researcher said he spent less time browsing, and that could possibly be a disadvantage.

Table 15. USE OF DELIVERY SERVICE TO MEET LIBRARY NEEDS

Frequency of use	n	%	% of Library needs met	n	%
Less than 1/month	11	19	0-5	8	14
Once/month	8	14	6-25	8	14
Twice/month	15	25	26-50	21	35
Once/week	13	22	51-75	15	25
More than once/week	12	20	76-100	7	12
	59	100		59	100

Overall, respondents' comments are probably the best indicator of the potential impact of such a service on its users. Three comments seem to sum up respondents' reactions to the service. One professor commented, "Delivery is efficient. When planning, I used to have to spend two or three hours at the library. Now, five minutes on the phone, and the next day the materials are delivered to you. I don't waste as much time." Another noted that he now tries to "plan ahead to take advantage of the efficiency of the service." Still another stated, "I'm more likely to use the library with the delivery service. I now look up things I might otherwise have neglected. It's like having an extra hour or two a day."

Another potentially far-reaching impact of improved document delivery access was cautiously stated by two individuals who noted that their expectation rates of locating materials had actually decreased since the advent of the delivery system. Their reactions represented a total departure from the established response pattern. However, their reactions were quite enlightening. Prior to the delivery service, few researchers bothered to frequent many of the branches located in out-of-the-way places; consequently, the persistent library user had almost free reign over those materials. With the availability of a delivery system, such materials are now easily accessible to those who beforehand had shunned them. As a result, the chances of retrieving those documents have actually decreased slightly. In other words, an inverse relationship exists between accessibility and availability. As accessibility increases, the availability of some documents will diminish. The relationship will affect overall library performance.

Results of the Study

Attitudes Toward Document Delivery During a Period of Tight Budgets. One way to measure the importance of a service is to ask users to evaluate it in a period of tight budgets. Those interviewed were asked to rate the importance of the service by selecting among the descriptors: essential, important, convenient or luxury. The results of the analysis are displayed in Table 16.

Table 16. EVALUATION OF THE DELIVERY SERVICE - OSU

Description	f	%*
Essential	11	19
Important	25	42
Convenient	28	47
Luxury	7	12

*Percents add up to more than 100 because some respondents used more than one term to describe the delivery service.

An attempt was made to cross-check the consistency of the replies by asking respondents to rate the service as a high, medium or low budgetary item in a time of tight dollars. It was felt that those who gave a high budget priority should also rate the service as essential or important, those who assigned a medium rating to the service should consider it of less importance to them, and those who ranked it as a low budget priority should be more likely to assign a least essential rating. The tabulation shown in Table 17 reflects a rather consistent pattern of responses.

Table 17. RATING OF BUDGET PRIORITY AND SERVICE UTILITY AS EXPRESSED BY USERS OF THE DELIVERY SERVICE

Service utility	High		Medium		Low		Total	
	n	%	n	%	n	%	n	%
Essential	9	15	2	3	0	0	11	18
Important	13	22	7	12	5	8	25	42
Convenient	7	12	12	20	9	15	28	47
Luxury	0	0	1	2	6	10	7	12

Over half of the respondents viewed the service as essential or important to their work. Only 12 percent labelled the service as a budgetary luxury. In a short period of time, the document delivery service has gained the support of the majority of its users. Moreover, as the service had been in effect for only a year, it is likely that as time passes and the information gathering habits of more users are affected, the service will rate even higher.

Document Delivery and Changes in Perceived Importance of the Library as a Source of Information. An increase in the importance of the library as a source of information, as perceived by users once they gain access to materials through the delivery system, represents one criterion by which to measure the service. At both institutions, those interviewed ranked the library as the second most important source of information. If the objective of the analysis had been to distinguish in absolute terms the library's importance among the other sources, the results would be highly suspect. While it would be comforting to librarians if users held the library in such high esteem, the conclusion would seem to contradict the findings of other researchers who have reported that printed sources and the library ranked relatively low among sources of information.[17] More realistically, the high rankings are probably contaminated by a halo effect. Because librarians were asking questions about libraries, some subjects may not have wanted to be critical of the library; others were simply pleased to have someone seek their opinion.

The mean rankings assigned by researchers in the two dissimilar environments were virtually identical (Table 18). A rank correlation comparing the reaction of the two groups produced an r value of 0.99.[18]

Subjects who used the document delivery service were unanimous in ranking the library as an important source of information. A chi square analysis of the difference between SU and OSU proved significant (Table 19). The researchers concluded that, regardless of the relative importance of the library among the alternative information sources, library users in the environment where a document delivery service was provided tended to attach greater importance to the library as a source of information than among users who must retrieve materials for themselves.

Table 18. COMPARISON OF MEAN RANKING OF SOURCES OF INFORMATION: SU and OSU

Syracuse University	x̄ Rank	Ohio State University	x̄ Rank
Personal collections	1.59	Personal collections	1.86
Univ. library system	2.70	Univ. library system	2.00
Conversation, on campus	3.65	Conversation, on campus	3.76
Papers at meetings	3.98	Papers at meetings	4.57
Conversation, off campus	4.01	Doctoral students	4.60
Colleagues' collections	4.06	Conversation, off campus	4.78
Doctoral students	4.14	Colleagues' collections	5.17
Dept'l reading room*	3.52	Dept'l reading room**	5.00

*Only 49 respondents had access to a departmental reading room. Of this number, 19 ranked it as important; 30 considered it unimportant.

**Total number of respondents with departmental reading room not known. Twenty (20) ranked it important; the corresponding percent value (39%) may not be the real value as this was obtained by dividing 20 by 59. Mean ranks for both SU and OSU are not comparable with other mean ranks as n (number of respondents with reading room) is not the same as total sample size.

Table 19. CHI SQUARE: RANKING OF THE LIBRARY AS A SOURCE OF INFORMATION: COMPARISON BETWEEN SU AND OSU USERS WHO RATED THE LIBRARY AS AN IMPORTANT SOURCE

Scale of Importance	SU	OSU	Totals
1	23	27	50
2	23	18	41
3	12	4	16
4	7	8	15
5-8	35	2	37
	100	59	159

$X^2 = 25.88$ (Significant at $_{.05}X^2_{df=4} = 9.49$).

COMPARISON OF SU AND OSU FACULTY ATTITUDES TOWARD DELIVERY SYSTEMS

The comparison of faculty attitudes between the two groups of subjects was crudely unambiguous. Attitudes of SU faculty interviewed toward the provision of a service for themselves and their colleagues proved to be much more negative than the attitudes exhibited by OSU faculty who already had the service available to them. A chi square analysis was extremely significant at the .05 level (Table 20).

Table 20. CHI SQUARE: SU AND OSU ATTITUDES TOWARD THE DESIRABILITY OF DOCUMENT DELIVERY FOR FACULTY

Attitude	SU Observed	OSU Observed	Totals
Strongly agree	15	36	51
Agree	32	21	53
Uncertain, disagree and strongly disagree	53	2	55
	100	59	159

$X^2 = 51.04$ (Significant at $_{.05}X^2_{df=2} = 5.99$)

As might be expected, the reaction of SU subjects to the suggestion that a delivery service be provided to graduate students was even more negative (Table 21). Generally, the majority of those interviewed believed that such a service would represent an unnecessary frill, that using the library should be part of the graduate student's learning experience and, finally, that such a service would be totally impractical in economic terms. Those who agreed with the suggestion usually spoke in terms of time saving and greater convenience to students. A chi square test of significance was performed to determine whether there was a difference in the attitudes observed. The analysis proved significant (Table 21).

The attitudes of faculty who had been exposed to the delivery service proved to be strikingly different from those who had not. An examination of the matrices in Table 22 shows clearly that the attitudes of those exposed are much

Results of the Study

more favorable toward delivery both to faculty as a group and also to graduate students. A distillation of the comments, pro and con, suggests that after actual use, faculty became more aware that the service saved them time and thus encouraged greater use of the library (See Appendices A-3 and D-2 for additional subjects' comments). Moreover, many subjects interviewed, especially at OSU, volunteered the opinion that in the long run the service would save the university money by increasing the productivity of its faculty. Those who disagreed, and there were not many (three percent), were, in the investigators' opinion, not so much expressing a negative view toward the service as they were conditioned by past practice. They were not convinced that such a service was really a necessity. However, even the detractors noted that they enjoyed the convenience of the delivery service.

Table 21. CHI SQUARE: ATTITUDES OF FACULTY TOWARD DELIVERY SERVICES FOR GRADUATE STUDENTS

Attitude	SU Observed	OSU Observed	Totals
Strongly agree	1	17	18
Agree	14	25	39
Uncertain	16	6	22
Disagree	43	9	52
Strongly disagree	26	2	28
	100	59	159

$X^2 = 39.6$ (Significant at $_{.05}X^2_{df=4} = 9.49$)

The reaction as to whether or not the delivery service privileges should be extended to students elicited many more negative comments in both environments. Basically, those who favored offering the service to graduate students (15 percent at SU and 72 percent at OSU) believed it would save their time in making materials more accessible. Those who would not support such a policy (69 percent at SU and 18 percent at OSU) usually expressed the view that the library experience is part of a graduate student's program. There was also manifest an extreme uneasiness about the economic implications of such a service. It should be pointed out that some of the faculty who expressed positive views toward offering a delivery service to graduate students did also suggest that the faculty should have preference if a choice had to be made. In summary, the attitudes expressed by faculty toward the delivery service for graduate students were not as favorable as for faculty colleagues. The attitudes at OSU were much more favorable than those expressed by faculty in the environment where no delivery service exists.

Table 22. COMPARISON BETWEEN SU AND OSU FACULTY ATTITUDES TOWARD DELIVERY SERVICE FOR THEMSELVES AND GRADUATE STUDENTS (in percent)*

A. SU FACULTY

		S.A.	A.	U.	D.	S.D.	Total
		\multicolumn{6}{c	}{STUDENTS}
A	S.A.	1	5	3	5	1	15
C	A.	0	9	10	11	2	32
U	U.	0	0	3	6	2	11
L	D.	0	0	0	21	15	36
T	S.D.	0	0	0	0	6	6
Y		1	14	16	43	26	100

B. OSU FACULTY

		S.A.	A.	U.	D.	S.D.	Total
		\multicolumn{6}{c	}{STUDENTS}
A	S.A.	27	26	3	2	3	61
C	A.	2	17	7	10	0	36
U	U.	0	0	0	0	0	0
L	D.	0	0	0	3	0	3
T	S.D.	0	0	0	0	0	0
Y		29	43	10	15	3	100

*In Table 22, SA = strongly agree; A = agree; U = undecided; D = disagree; SD = strongly disagree.

<u>OSU Non-Users' Attitudes Toward Delivery</u>. The responses of the eight non-users of the delivery service from

Results of the Study

the OSU faculty were very similar to the responses of those interviewed in the SU sample. The mean expectation rate was 5.0; the expectations ranged from four to nine, and the distribution was bimodal with two peaks at five and seven (Figure 5). In answer to the query concerning attitudes toward the availability of a delivery service, the answers tended to be less favorable in relation to offering the service to faculty and rather negative in relation to graduate students. The summary of responses is shown in Table 23.

Table 23. REACTION OF OSU NON-USERS TO PROVISION OF A DELIVERY SERVICE TO FACULTY AND GRADUATE STUDENTS

Reaction	Service to Faculty	Service to Graduate Students
Strongly agree	1	0
Agree	4	2
Uncertain	2	1
Disagree	1	3
Strongly disagree	0	2
Total	8	8

A composite profile of a researcher favoring delivery services could be summarized in the following way: (1) he believes that a delivery service would prove to be a time saver and would make the library more convenient to use; (2) he would be able to reduce frustrations in using the library; and, (3) overall, the service would give him more time for his other academic pursuits--teaching, counseling and research.

On the other hand, those who expressed unfavorable attitudes toward delivery service for faculty (42 percent at SU and three percent at OSU) would have a different set of values. They would be more likely to feel that delivery service was a poor use of library funds; they would prefer to see the monies used to purchase additional materials. They would claim that faculty should know how to use the library themselves and would place greater importance on browsing.* They would tend to believe that a delivery service was not essential; thus, they would place less value on the expenditure of faculty time.

The reflected attitudes toward a delivery service should not be interpreted to imply that those who viewed such a service favorably were better teachers or better researchers than those who expressed negative reactions; only that the faculty working in different environments--some close to, some far away from the library, some relying heavily on literature, some not--have evolved different sets of values. There was no relationship among disciplines, i.e., humanities, social sciences and sciences, and attitudes toward the delivery service. The reactions, both positive and negative, seemed to cut across subject areas at random.

SUMMARY

The findings of the investigation reported in this chapter may be summarized as follows:

1. Library materials of potential relevance to individual faculty researchers were dispersed throughout several locations in the Syracuse University campus library system.

2. The number of libraries Syracuse University faculty researchers frequented is far below the number of libraries housing potentially relevant materials.

3. Decentralized branch library organization at Syracuse University did not minimize the number of library locations faculty had to consult to gain access to materials of potential interest to them.

4. The library use pattern of SU faculty did not appear to be influenced by the percentage of relevant documents housed in any one specific location.

5. There was no relationship between an individual Syracuse University faculty researcher's expectation rate and

---

*The investigators gained the impression that some of those who emphasized the importance of browsing had heard a rumor that a delivery service might cause them to lose direct stack access.

Results of the Study

his document exposure index. In other words, depth of holdings in the library or libraries an individual reportedly frequents is not a predictor of that individual's expectation of successfully obtaining materials from the library system.

6. The distance of a Syracuse University researcher's office from the libraries he used was a more positive predictor of his expectation rate than was the richness, or lack thereof, of holdings in the libraries used.

7. Syracuse University faculty who used branch libraries exhibited a much higher expectation rate than those who used the central library.

8. Ohio State University faculty have a higher expectation rate with access to library materials through a document delivery service than they claimed to have had before the introduction of the service.

9. Ohio State University faculty who have access to library materials via a document delivery service reported a higher expectation rate than Syracuse University faculty who do not have access through a delivery service.

10. At both Syracuse University and Ohio State University, an individual who was successful in obtaining materials on his last visit to the library tended to harbor more positive feelings toward the library than an individual who was unsuccessful on his last use of the library system.

11. Ohio State University faculty harbored very positive attitudes toward the document delivery service and reported that the service had improved accessibility of library materials and had increased their use of library resources.

12. Ohio State University library users in an environment where a document delivery service was provided tended to attach greater importance to the library as a source of information than Syracuse University users who had to retrieve materials for themselves.

13. The attitudes of Ohio State University researchers toward the desirability of a document delivery service for both faculty and students were much more positive than the attitudes of Syracuse University researchers who have not had access to a delivery service.

In short, the investigators found that despite the concentration of similar materials in branch locations, materials of potential relevance to an individual faculty researcher were dispersed through more locations than the individual used. Thus, the branch library structure may well have impeded an individual's access to all relevant materials. On the other hand, attitudes of users of branch libraries were generally more positive toward the library as a source of information than attitudes of users of the central library. In addition, Ohio State University faculty who used the document delivery service held much more favorable attitudes toward the library as an information source and were very enthusiastic about the value of a document delivery service for faculty and graduate students. In contrast, SU faculty who had no experience with a library delivery service were quite negative concerning the value of delivery services to both themselves and graduate students.

Notes

15. Berelson, Bernard, The Library's Public. New York: Columbia University Press, 1949, pp. 43-6.

16. Letter from Larry X. Besant, Assistant Director of Libraries for Public Services, Ohio State University, July 19, 1972.

17. Fishenden, R. M., "Methods by which research workers find information," In: International Conference on Scientific Proceedings, Washington, D.C. (Nov. 16-21, 1959), pp. 169-79.

18. Spearman rank order correlation (rho) found in Bruning, James L. and B. L. Kintz, Computational Handbook of Statistics, Glenview, Illinois: Scott Foresman, 1968, pp. 152-5.

Chapter IV

OTHER FINDINGS OF THE INVESTIGATION

It was recognized at the outset that there are a number of related variables affecting the attitudes of faculty and their use of a university library system. Other variables mentioned earlier include the environment of the library, the service orientation of the library staff, availability of parking facilities, and the quality of the collections. Because of the potential importance on library organization and services, the investigators queried the faculty on other matters: first, the role played by the library in connection with course work; second, the faculty attitudes toward departmental reading rooms; third, the incidence of faculty delegating document retrieval problems to others; fourth, the incidence of change in faculty's research interests and the similarity between their research interests and their teaching responsibilities; and fifth, the role doctoral students play in the communication network within an academic department. The remainder of the report summarizes briefly the data gathered in connection with such topics.

LIBRARY USE AND TEACHING

Faculty members interviewed who stated that the library was an important source of information were more likely to use library resources in connection with at least one of their courses than those who stated that the library was an unimportant source of information. A chi square analysis produced a significant finding (Table 24).

The significance of the statistical analysis was encouraging. However, analysis of the anecdotal comments produced a picture which was educationally depressing. The best that could be said is that those faculty who were using the library used it in a superficial manner. It was apparent from the responses of SU faculty that independent study or self-directed education remains a promise unfulfilled. A tabulation summarizing the ways in which faculty said they were using the library revealed that a majority still limit their library activity to placing books on reserve either as required or supplementary readings (Table 25). Others assigned papers which they believed (or assumed) required students to use the library as a source of background information. Others provided students with recommended or supplementary readings which may or may not be placed on reserve.

Table 24. CHI SQUARE: PERCEIVED IMPORTANCE OF LIBRARY AND USE OF THE LIBRARY IN TEACHING

Uses Library for Course Work	Important	Unimportant	Totals
Yes	57	6	63
No	21	16	37
Totals	78	22	100

$X^2 = 13.5$ (Significant at $_{.95}X^2_{1df} = 3.84$)
$C = .49$

Table 25. TYPES OF LIBRARY USE IN SUPPORT OF COURSES

Type of Use	f
Reserved reading	42
Term papers (research papers)	30
Use of special forms of materials as part of project or background reading:	
(1) journals	11
(2) phonorecords	4
(3) scores	3
(4) microfilms	1
(5) reference books	3
Supplementary readings listed in class reading lists, course syllabi or suggested in lectures:	
(1) reading lists, syllabi, bibliographies	15
(2) lectures	13

Other Findings

Without exception, none of the faculty members interviewed provided the investigators with an articulated plan which integrated the resources of the library into a formal course. The investigators were left with the distinct impression that the library, in fact, formed only a peripheral aspect of the teaching program.

DEPARTMENTAL READING ROOMS

In most university environments, departmental reading rooms are customarily operated by academic teaching departments.* Departmental reading rooms are generally supported through donations, either monetary or material, from members of the faculty, from departmental supply budgets, or from research grant overheads. If staffed at all, the rooms are entrusted to the care of the secretarial staff and/or graduate students. In some instances, the reading room is acknowledged to play an important role within the department. In others, it plays a tangential or peripheral role. The basic question which remains unanswered is what role an optimally equipped departmental reading room could play as a source of information to teachers and researchers. It is possible, but still speculation, that some researchers use branch libraries in much the same way as others use departmental reading rooms; that is, the reading room is a place to house materials for classes, to keep abreast of the key professional journals, and to provide a meeting place where members of the department can exchange face-to-face communication.

In the investigation, Syracuse University subjects were asked whether or not their department operated a reading room. Of the 100 faculty interviewed, 49 acknowledged the presence of such a facility. Of the 49, 59 percent stated that they used the facility themselves and 43 percent related at least some of their classroom assignments to materials housed in the reading room. Twenty-six percent stated that they did not use the reading room at all because it did not contain enough materials of interest to them (See Appendix A-3). The data in Table 26 summarize briefly the purposes

---

*The University of British Columbia Libraries began to support collection development and cataloging of materials located in departmental reading rooms in 1970 (Annual Report of the Librarian). The impact of the policy on service is not known.

to which the reading rooms are used.

Table 26. SELECTED USES OF DEPARTMENTAL READING ROOMS

	FUNCTION	
Type of Use	Teaching f	Research f
Shelves personal materials	3	
Shelves library reserves	3	
Places supplementary classroom materials	3	
Uses texts and reference materials		11
Current awareness reading		3
Regular class readings	6	

It was apparent from the comments that a reading room can serve a variety of functions. For some, it represented a way to avoid the frustrations associated with a large library system, in that they could make readings for students more accessible. For others, the reading room was a place in which they were more willing to place their own materials on reserve, apparently because they were more confident of their security. Some subjects used the reading room as a source of reference information. Others interviewed stated that they read the journals which were purchased by the department to keep abreast of their fields.

Because the data were subjective, no claim could be made for their reliability. Nonetheless, the investigators were convinced that the role of and potential importance of reading rooms are but barely understood. The investigators believe that further research on the question is definitely warranted.

WHO RETRIEVES MATERIALS FROM THE LIBRARY?

Generally, it has been assumed that the faculty are skilled users of the library; at least, they are supposed to

Other Findings

comprise the most sophisticated group of users--and well they may. On the other hand, the skills of researchers who frequent libraries which house only a fraction of the materials of relevance to them are suspect (Table 7). Furthermore, does the researcher retrieve materials for himself, or is this chore assigned to an assistant?

The faculty interviewed were asked whether or not they retrieved their own materials from the library, and if not, who did retrieve them. Seventy-nine percent of the OSU faculty and 89 percent of the SU faculty retrieved their own documents from the library at least some of the time. In both environments, about 40 percent of those interviewed acknowledged that on some occasions they did send someone else to the library. A breakdown is shown in Table 27.

Table 27. LIBRARY MATERIAL RETRIEVAL PATTERNS - SU AND OSU

	SU %*	OSU %*
Goes himself	89	79
Sends secretary	4	8
Sends graduate assistant	42	17
Sends undergraduate	15	17
Sends others	5	3

*Adds up to more than 100% because several respondents reported sending more than one category of individual to retrieve materials.

The faculty seemed to have confidence in those who retrieved materials for them. As shown in Table 28, faculty expressed the same or higher ERs in 89 percent of the categories cited. The usual explanation cited for the higher ER was that others were sent only when the item was known to be available.

Table 28. PERSON SENT TO THE LIBRARY BY SUBJECT
AND HIS EXPECTATION RATE -
SYRACUSE UNIVERSITY*

Classification of Person Sent	Number	Expectation Rate When Someone Sent			
		The Same	Different	Higher	Lower
Secretary	4	3	1	1	
Research Assistant	11	6	5	4	1
Graduate Assistant	31	19	12	9	3
Student Employee	0	-	-	-	-
Undergraduate	15	8	7	3	4
Other	5	2	3	3	
Total	66	38	28	20	8

*Some interviewees cited more than one category.

CHANGING FACULTY RESEARCH INTERESTS

A few faculty members interviewed during the pilot study revealed a major change in their current research interest from their previous years' work. In fact, two indicated that their past research endeavors were totally unrelated to the subject field in which they were presently concentrating their research efforts. In order to develop complete subject interest profiles, the investigators felt it was necessary to look into possible changes with the 100 SU faculty interviewed. When asked if the courses they taught during the current academic year and/or their past publications reflected their current research pursuits, 59 percent of the SU faculty noted that, indeed, their present research differed markedly from their past interests. The incidence of change in research interests was not as great among the 59 Ohio State faculty interviewed: 20 percent reported that their publications of the past five years did not reflect their current research interests and 22 percent noted that courses taught were also unrelated to their current research efforts.

The potential impact of such shifts in interests was not investigated, but if changing research interests are a universal phenomenon, many questions should be answered. What information needs are created, and may be unserved,

Other Findings 73

by such shifts in research interests? Is it possible for librarians to anticipate and identify such shifts in order to meet changing information needs? Does a change in a faculty member's research interests portend a change in the instructional program? If so, how soon? It is the opinion of the investigators that additional research on the topic is warranted.

DOCTORAL STUDENTS IN THE ROLE OF COMMUNICATION GATE KEEPERS

Thomas Allen, several years ago, published the results of a study which shed a great deal of light on how information was transmitted among several research and development teams working to solve the same problem.[19] Allen identified several distinguishing characteristics of individuals who tended to serve as communication gate keepers for the groups. Three of the characteristics are: (1) such individuals had greater contact with technical people outside of the organization; (2) they were more exposed to the technical literature; and (3) they relied more heavily upon internal consultations.

Decision-makers in academia, foundations and governmental agencies have traditionally given most attention to the academic stars when funding information systems. A "star" here is defined as a person who has achieved a level of success within his discipline and is highly respected by his colleagues, administrative officials and doctoral students. It is not surprising, then, that it has been the academic stars in whose hands the principal responsibility for developing innovative non-traditional information systems has been vested. Paradoxically, though, the "stars" may be exactly the ones who need such services least. It is the academic stars who have alternative sources of information; that is, they can place greater reliance upon verbal communication and have access to one or more invisible colleges. By contrast, it is the young, unestablished researchers who have least access to outside sources and, thus, have the greatest need to retrieve information from printed sources.

The doctoral student working on his own research may represent an important link in the academic department's communication chain. It may be doctoral students who are most familiar with the published literature inasmuch as they must gain a command of the literature as one task in their research projects. The question is, what is the doctoral student's role in the communication process within his department, among his peers and with his advisor?

It was the investigators' hypothesis that doctoral students frequently play a heretofore unappreciated role as communication gate keepers. Time did not permit the development of a reliable methodology which would clearly define the role.

Subjects were queried as to whether or not they perceived doctoral students as an important source of information. An examination of Table 18 shows that doctoral students did not rate high as a source of information in comparison to other sources.* However, 49 percent of those interviewed at SU and 44 percent of the subjects at OSU attached some importance to doctoral students as sources. Furthermore, a close examination of the data revealed that ten out of 50 people (17 percent) interviewed at OSU ranked doctoral students as one of their top three sources, and 18 percent of the faculty at SU ranked doctoral students similarly.

Moreover, when queried about doctoral candidates' roles as a source of information, many subjects were caught completely unprepared. They obviously had never given any thought to doctoral students as communication gate keepers. As they mulled over the question, it began to dawn on them that one or more of their doctoral students indeed served as sources of ideas and information. In the opinion of the researchers, additional research on the topic is definitely warranted.

SUMMARY

Additional findings of the investigation may be summarized as follows:

1. Syracuse University faculty who stated the library was an important source of information were more likely to

---

*Because several departments do not offer doctoral programs, some responses recorded as "not important" would have been more accurately recorded as "not applicable." In other words, the importance of doctoral students is definitely understated.

Other Findings

use library resources in connection with the courses they taught than faculty members who viewed the library as an unimportant source of information.

2. Syracuse University faculty reported very superficial use of library resources in relation to their instructional programs: reserve readings, supplementary readings, and assigned term papers.

3. Syracuse University faculty varied in their use of and opinion of departmental reading rooms. The investigators did not obtain a clear picture of the actual or potential role and importance of the departmental reading room in meeting the information needs of faculty interviewed.

4. Although more than three-fourths of the Syracuse University and Ohio State University faculty members interviewed went to the library to retrieve their own materials at least some of the time, almost half of them also sent other people to obtain documents for them.

5. Current courses taught and past publications do not necessarily reflect the current research interests of many Syracuse University and Ohio State University faculty interviewed.

6. Almost half of the Syracuse University and Ohio State University faculty interviewed considered doctoral students as an important source of information.

Note

19. Allen, T. J., "Organizational aspects of information flow and technology; with discussion," ASLIB Proceedings, Vol. 20 (November, 1968), pp. 433-54.

Chapter V

FINDINGS, CONCLUSIONS AND IMPLICATIONS

One of the initial objectives of the investigation was to examine the influence of campus library organizational structure on the document delivery effectiveness of the library. First, the study postulated that within the context of traditional library and information systems, there may be an irreconcilable separation between the physical location of informational sources and the persons who require information. A second corollary hypothesis was that, in a period dominated by interdisciplinary studies, traditional decentralized (i.e., departmental branches) library systems do not offer researchers easy accessibility to relevant information. Third, it was hypothesized that decentralized systems do not increase user satisfaction nor achieve a high utilization of information resources. A fourth postulate was that an academic library system could increase user satisfaction, based on users' perceptions of the library, and achieve greater utilization of its resources through the introduction of some type of document delivery system.

LIBRARY USERS AND THE DISPERSION OF MATERIALS

The number of libraries housing documents of potential relevance to individual researchers ranged from one to thirteen. The mean number of libraries housing relevant documents for the entire sample was slightly more than seven. The data presented in Table 7 show clearly that materials of potential interest to researchers working in the humanities were often concentrated in one library (usually about 90 percent) with only a small percentage of the total holdings scattered in additional branches. In marked contrast to the humanities, however, were the dispersion patterns observed in the social, natural and applied sciences. Researchers in these disciplines must consult more than four libraries in order to gain access to an equal percentage of library holdings. The data collected in the investigation support the

Findings, Conclusions and Implications 77

conclusion that library materials of potential relevance to individual faculty researchers are likely to be scattered among several locations in the campus library system.

The Syracuse University faculty sampled do not use all of the libraries which housed documents of potential interest to them. The mean number of libraries housing documents was seven, whereas the mean number of libraries actually used was two. Therefore, many documents housed in the university library system are virtually inaccessible to the individual, simply because the materials are not located in his preferred library outlets. Thus, the data support the conclusion that the organization of the Syracuse University Library system, a commonly encountered organizational pattern for academic libraries, in effect has created a schism between the physical location of its documents and the people who need the information contained in the resources.

Traditionally, branch libraries have been established on university campuses in order to improve the accessibility of materials to specific groups of users. But it was found in the investigation that even when a branch was provided, the materials relevant to the branch's stated scope of subject coverage were widely dispersed throughout the system. The poor match observed among users, materials and branches was particularly evident among the sciences. All but five of the 24 researchers interviewed from the sciences had access to a branch library associated with their disciplines. Nonetheless, all of those sampled had to consult a minimum of four different locations to achieve full exposure to documents of interest, and in many cases their materials were scattered among up to 12 different locations.

The comparison between the observed mean document exposure index (DEI) scores for researchers who have a branch associated with their discipline and the DEI scores of researchers in departments without a branch library also disputed the belief that branch libraries provide greater physical access to relevant materials. In the investigation, no significant difference in the mean DEI scores was observed--$\bar{X} = 82.6$ (branch) and $\bar{X} = 83.4$ (no branch). The DEI scores do not consider the user's concern for convenience, only the individual's total exposure to documents of potential interest. The SU data support the conclusion that the concentration of relevant materials through decentralization may not significantly improve the user's access to potentially relevant materials.

Although library use patterns did not appear to be influenced by the proportion of relevant documents housed at a specific location, the distance from a researcher's office to libraries housing documents of interest, did seem to influence his choice of libraries. Users tended to avoid libraries which were a great distance away. In fact, the investigators observed that faculty with offices located at the center of the campus (the quad) tended to move freely among libraries located on the quad, but were less prone to frequent libraries which necessitated leaving their immediate campus location, or libraries which would necessitate driving cars and searching anew for parking spaces. One notable exception to the observed tendency was the apparent willingness of some faculty to go to a nearby medical library which is located on the fringe of the main campus, not within easy walking distance and in a congested traffic area. The reasons cited for its use were stronger holdings arranged in a more convenient manner, and a greater probability that the desired item would be available for use. Nonetheless, the data do seem to support the conclusion that distance is a variable which influences a researcher's choice of libraries: the nearer the library, the more likely he is to use it.

It would appear from the findings that many researchers place greater importance on the convenience of access to library collections than they do on comprehensiveness of holdings. There are several possibilities why comprehensiveness of holdings is not a strong influence on the choice of libraries used. Researchers may be unaware that they are missing materials of potential relevance; they may be already suffering from an information overload and are not interested in increasing the number of documents they scan; or a librarian may compensate for the lack of holdings by acquiring needed materials from other branches on request. Several of the faculty using branch libraries commented on the efficiency and willingness of their librarians to provide special "retrieval" services. Then, too, the smaller and more personal environment of a branch library is more familiar, less threatening, more inviting and more convenient. The proprietary feeling faculty have toward their branch libraries is well known.

The desire for convenience and accessibility explains, in part, why researchers usually opposed a library's attempt to disband a branch collection. In short, a user's desire for convenience is in direct opposition to a library director's need to achieve a high level of operational efficiency. However,

Findings, Conclusions and Implications

the outcome of a user's last recorded library experience on user attitudes suggests that it might be possible for a library to regain, if not retain, the goodwill of faculty while increasing centralization, if it can demonstrate alternative, effective methods of access to library collections. In this regard, a library might offer an array of new services just at the time it plans to announce the decision to centralize some or all of its collections, in an attempt to offset or counteract adverse criticism precipitated by the decision to centralize.

USER ATTITUDES TOWARD LIBRARY EFFECTIVENESS: EXPECTATION RATINGS

Because the investigators believed that a user's perceptions of a library system's effectiveness may well be more important than the system's actual ability to meet his information needs, the study attempted to measure the subjective opinions of researchers toward the library in two different environments--one with and one without a document delivery service. The primary focus was to identify how a researcher's subjective attitudes influenced his library usage.

One notable finding was that no relationship was observed between the percentage of total holdings of potential relevance housed in the first-used library and the user's expectation rate (ER). In other words, completeness of holdings, or lack thereof, in the user's preferred library was not a powerful predictor of his ER. On the other hand, a significant difference was observed between the ERs of SU subjects who reported satisfaction with their last library use and those who reported dissatisfaction. The mean ER of those who reported satisfaction was 7.0 while the mean ER of those who were dissatisfied was 4.3. An almost identical pattern was noted among the OSU subjects interviewed: the mean ER of satisfied users was 7.82 whereas an ER of 6.12 was observed for dissatisfied users. The investigators concluded that the outcome of an individual's last recorded use influenced his general attitude toward the library.

Although the configuration of branch library organization did not increase user accessibility to potentially relevant materials, the availability of branches did influence user ERs. The mean ERs of SU faculty whose first-used library was a branch was 7.0 compared to a mean ER of 5.1 for those whose first-used library was the central library. Despite the dispersion of relevant materials throughout the system, it was obvious that, in the test environment, faculty exhibited a greater confidence that they could retrieve desired documents from a branch library than from the central collection. It is also obvious that the greater perceived effectiveness of branches must be derived from factors other than the concentration of holdings. Again, anecdotal data elicited from faculty would indicate the importance of convenience of location, an accessible and service-oriented branch librarian, and ease of becoming familiar with a smaller branch collection as influential factors.

Distance also affected users' expectation rates. An analysis of variance of the SU subjects' ERs, in relation to the distance from office to first-choice library, revealed that user proximity to a library was a better predictor of ERs than was the concentration, or lack thereof, of holdings in that library.

The mean ER for researchers from the sciences was 6.96; for the social sciences, 5.00; and for the humanities, 5.91. Because each group comprised less than 50 people, the investigators were reluctant to draw specific conclusions pertaining to differences along discipline lines in the observed attitudes toward library effectiveness. Questions do arise as to whether the ERs differ as a result of an individual's association with a specific academic department or group of departments, and if so, why. Also, are such differences a result of a localized situation or typical of the groups in various academic settings? Further probes would seem warranted.

While decentralization of collections did not appear to increase the overall user DEI scores, the higher ERs expressed by researchers who used branch libraries, plus the positive relationship identified between ER and distance, suggest that user satisfaction toward a library system will be increased as the system is decentralized. One important question which requires further research is the trade-off between convenience of access and the frustrations caused by collection fragmentation.

The importance a user attached to the library as a source of information was found to be positively related to his ER. The mean ER for SU faculty who judged the library important was 6.18, whereas a mean ER of 4.77 was expressed by those who considered the library unimportant as a source of information. The investigators concluded that

Findings, Conclusions and Implications 81

users' attitudes do affect their use of the library system. In short, they will be more likely to consult the library for materials if they believe there is a reasonable expectation of success and if they consider the library to be an important source of information to support teaching and research activities.

A comparison of SU faculty ERs with those of the OSU faculty both before and after the latter's use of the delivery service supports the conclusion that a document delivery service will contribute to a more positive attitude toward a library. The OSU faculty users of the delivery service exhibited a mean ER of 7.6, while the same individuals reported a mean ER of 5.0 prior to using the delivery service, which was quite similar to the mean ER of the SU faculty (5.76). The importance attached to the library as a source of information was significantly greater for OSU subjects who had used the delivery service than for SU subjects who had not had the benefit of a similar service.

One note of caution must be reiterated. The on-line circulation system introduced at OSU a little more than a year before has also had a tremendous impact on the attitudes and behavior of the subjects interviewed. The new circulation system has rendered a change on the library use patterns of many users. The investigators were not always able to distinguish between the effect of the two services. Nonetheless, the two services in combination have made it easier to obtain information about books as well as the books themselves; the preponderance of the evidence supports the conclusion that the delivery system has had a positive influence on user attitudes.

COMPARISON BETWEEN USERS' AND NON-USERS' ATTITUDES TOWARD DOCUMENT DELIVERY

The investigators were most interested in learning how the use of a delivery service might affect the attitudes of users toward it, in comparison with the attitudes of individuals who were never exposed to the service. When presented with the theoretical proposition, 97 percent of those interviewed at OSU agreed that faculty should be able to have documents delivered to them, while only 47 percent agreed at SU. The difference was found to be statistically significant. Furthermore, in an analysis of the comments elicited in support of a delivery service, SU faculty expressed more reservations about the feasibility, the need, and the priority of a delivery service, whereas the OSU faculty tended to view it as both an important library service and a convenient one.

A similar spread in attitudes toward delivery services for graduate students was observed between the two groups, with 72 percent of the OSU faculty and only 15 percent of the SU faculty in favor of it. Those objecting to the service for graduate students not only expressed concern about costs and the logistical feasibility, but also felt that a graduate student's experience should include learning to retrieve his own materials from the library. Quite obviously, individuals who were familiar with a service were more apt to view it as important. In short, their personal experiences, or lack thereof, affected their evaluation of the service. Apparently, Syracuse University faculty did not miss what they never had, while OSU faculty hated to give up what they had enjoyed for only a brief time.

The differences in attitudes observed can be partially explained by the fact that both groups based their responses on current library experiences and perceptions as to what constitutes library service. An understanding of the process of innovation diffusion will account for the behavioral changes one can expect to observe after a new service has been introduced.

USERS' ATTITUDES TOWARD AN INNOVATIVE LIBRARY SERVICE: DOCUMENT DELIVERY

The fourth hypothesis of the investigation stated that a library could increase user satisfaction with library effectiveness and achieve greater utilization of its resources by making a document delivery system available to its users. The data left no doubt that faculty users of the delivery service were enthusiastic about its positive value to them. Ninety-three percent rated it as a good or excellent service, and 41 percent gave the service a "high" priority in times of tight budgets. Very few (seven percent) of the faculty interviewed, who had used the service, felt that it represented an unnecessary frill. Quite the contrary, the service frequently had become an integral component in the user's information gathering process.

Users of the delivery service also expressed the opinion that the service had increased the collection's accessi-

Findings, Conclusions and Implications

bility. Sixty-eight percent stated that the service had prompted them to increase the number of documents which they were now able to examine. When asked why, the almost universal response was that the collection was now more accessible and that the library was more convenient to use. In addition, because books were delivered to them as a result of a phone call, they did not have to contend with the inconvenience and frustrations of using many widely scattered branches. The data support the conclusion that among the users interviewed, the introduction of the document delivery system has resulted in more positive user attitudes toward the library and has increased their exploitation of the library's resources. Furthermore, if document delivery increases accessibility to library collections, then the service should decrease the justification and need for library branches.

INNOVATION DIFFUSION

The process of innovation diffusion has been studied by many investigators. A well-written overview of the discipline has been prepared by Rogers.[20] Based on the data, the investigators concluded that the behavioral patterns exhibited by the OSU and SU subjects toward a new idea were consonant with the process of diffusion observed in other disciplines.

The implications to librarians who plan to introduce new services are quite clear. First, one can assume the potential users will not even know of the existence of a new service unless an effective marketing campaign is mounted. Second, new services will not become a routine characteristic of a user's behavior until he is convinced that the new service is worth the effort he associates with change. For some users, only repeated uses will produce a behavioral change. Third, when individuals are asked to express their opinions about a service which is new to them, their answers will probably reflect past training and current experience. The striking change in attitudes toward document delivery underscores the risk of basing decision-making on the opinions of individuals who can speak only in the abstract. Fourth, new services must be planned and introduced to allow time for adequate diffusion. Funding should be provided for a period of time to ensure that the new service has been adopted. For example, funding of automated information systems for purposes of demonstration over a short period run a high risk of failure because there will have been inadequate time for the new service to be recognized, tried and adopted.

THE ROLE OF THE LIBRARY IN THE TEACHING PROGRAM

Although 63 percent of the subjects interviewed at SU reported that the library played an important role in at least one of the courses they taught, the investigators nevertheless concluded that the library is serving only a peripheral role in the teaching programs of those interviewed. The contribution of the library seemed to be limited to serving as a repository for reserve readings. Some individuals interviewed pointed out that they do assign papers to students, but the assignments were not designed to require students to consult library resources. Faculty only assumed that students used the library as a source of information.

Only the most tenuous of conclusions can be reached based on the experiences observed on a single campus, particularly because the present SU library staff must provide services in a building that is badly obsolete. It is an unattractive, dreary place to work. Once the library moves into its new quarters, an entirely new atmosphere may be created.

Nevertheless, the library at present is playing only a minimal role in the educational activity of the instructors interviewed. Many instructors have developed alternate sources of information. The prime sources include personal collections, collections of colleagues, paperbacks, and the resources of departmental reading rooms.

The argument of the library for adequate budget support, particularly during times of dollar shortages, is seriously weakened if the library serves only a peripheral role in the educational process. One might suggest that the most potent weapon against budget cutbacks is to become the indispensible source of information and services.

FACULTY RETRIEVAL OF LIBRARY MATERIALS

Fifty percent of the SU researchers interviewed and 36 percent of the OSU researchers interviewed send assistants to the library on some occasions to retrieve materials for them. The investigation did not attempt to determine if faculty are effective as document retrievers. The investigation attempted only to identify the extent to which others are involved in the faculty's document retrieval process.

Findings, Conclusions and Implications

Because numerous faculty do depend upon others to assist them in locating materials, libraries should consider seriously the need to provide instruction on library use to individuals such as graduate assistants, teaching assistants, undergraduates, and secretaries who are expected to perform as document retrievers as part of their job responsibilities. After all, the library's effectiveness will be assessed by faculty partly on the basis of the percentage of materials which are retrieved by their assistants.

DOCTORAL STUDENTS AS COMMUNICATION GATE KEEPERS

Doctoral students may function in a heretofore little-recognized role as communication gate keepers within academic departments. Forty-nine percent of the SU and 44 percent of the OSU faculty stated that doctoral students were an important source of information. Eighteen percent of the SU researchers interviewed ranked doctoral students as one of the three most important sources of information to them. Based on the initial reactions of many researchers interviewed, the investigators concluded that those queried were not consciously aware of the contributions their students rendered to them as disseminators of information.

The conclusions reached by the investigators are tentative. Nevertheless, the results are sufficiently positive to suggest additional research. Doctoral students may comprise a key link in the academic department's communication network. Students may also serve as "information" opinion leaders. In other words, students could serve as important allies to librarians in convincing other students and faculty of the potential benefits of such new services as automated information systems. The data gathered suggested that those attempting to introduce new information systems into an academic environment should enlist the support of doctoral students in marketing the new services.

SUMMARY

After analyzing the data collected on both the Syracuse University and Ohio State University campuses, the investigators concluded:

1. That the decentralized organization of the Syracuse University library system, a commonly encountered organiza-

tional structure for academic libraries, tends to erect a barrier between the physical location of its documents and the researchers who require the information contained in the library's resources;

2. That the concentration of related materials in various branch outlets does not appear to increase Syracuse University library system users' access to potentially relevant materials;

3. That many Syracuse University researchers place greater importance upon the ease of use and convenience of access to the library collection than they do upon the depth range of holdings in a preferred library location;

4. That decentralization of collections at Syracuse University does not contribute to greater utilization of information resources but does contribute to a higher degree of satisfaction with the library system as an information resource.

Because of the small and highly selective sample of Ohio State University faculty, no generalizable conclusions may be stated relative to the efficacy of the document delivery service introduced only a year previous to the study. The investigators urge anyone who is considering the inception of such an innovative service to initiate also a before-after study in order to establish base-line measures for evaluation purposes. Nonetheless, it is the opinion of the investigators that the introduction of the document delivery service at Ohio State University did appear to:

1. increase user satisfaction with the library system;
2. increase users' access to the library's collections;
3. contribute to greater utilization of library resources.

Therefore, it would appear that the inception of a document delivery service may tend to make the library organizational structure irrelevant in terms of users' expectations, access and utilization of the information resources.

Note

20. Rogers, Everett M., Diffusion of Innovations, New York: The Free Press of Glencoe, 1962, p. 34.

APPENDICES

Appendix A-1

SYRACUSE UNIVERSITY
APPOINTMENT PHONE CALL

"Hello, Prof. or Dr. _____. This is _____. The Library School has a National Science Foundation grant to study faculty utilization of information sources, and you are one of our sample members. May we make an appointment to interview you in the next week? It will take about 15 to 20 minutes."

After setting time and date for interview, ask if he would please have copies of his reading lists for various courses and a list of his publications (and speeches) of the last five years ready for interviewer. Offer to Xerox if he indicates it is a problem.

Appendix A-2

SYRACUSE UNIVERSITY
INTERVIEW INSTRUMENT

Name _____ Dept. _____ Rank _____
Campus Address _____ Degree _____
Branch Library _____

1. Do you usually go to the library yourself to get a specific item? (An item is defined as a book, periodical, document, etc.).
   ____yes   ____no

2. Do you ever send anyone else to the library to get a specific item?
   ____yes   ____no

3. If answer to question 2 is yes, who goes to the library for you?
   ____secretary
   ____research assistant (both student and staff)
   ____graduate assistant (just a student)
   ____student employee
   ____undergraduate student
   ____other (specify)
   _____

4. Which libraries on campus do you use?
   a. _____ ( )   d. _____ ( )
   b. _____ ( )   e. _____ ( )
   c. _____ ( )   f. _____ ( )

5. Would you rank the libraries you use in order of the frequency you use them? (Fill in the Blanks above.)

6a. Is there a reading room (not official part of university library system) organized and run by your department?
   ____yes   ____no

6b. Where is it located? _____

7. If yes, do you use the departmental reading room yourself or give student assignments in materials stocked there?
   _____ uses himself   _____ gives assignments
   Comment: _____
   _____
   _____

8a. When you need a specific item from the library, what would you estimate as your <u>expectation</u> that when you leave the library you will have that item in hand? _____

   (Rate your expectation from 0-10, with 5 interpreted to mean that you expect to locate the item half of the time, and 10 all of the time.)

   b. When you need a specific item from the library and you send your <u>secretary</u>, what would you estimate as your expectation that when he/she leaves the library, he/she will have the item in hand? _____

   c. Repeat question for graduate assistant. _____

   d. Repeat question for research assistant. _____

   e. Repeat question for student employee. _____

   f. Repeat question for undergraduate student. _____

   g. Repeat question for "other" (specify). _____

9. When you last tried to find a specific item, were you
   _____ satisfied
   _____ dissatisfied
   _____ don't remember
   with the results?

10. Do you organize your courses to include student use of the library system?
    _____ yes   _____ no
    Comments: _____
    _____
    _____
    _____

Appendices

11. Of the following sources, which ones do you consider important sources of information for your teaching and research? ("Information" is defined here to include bibliographic citations, document retrieval, ideas and concepts, latest research and development in his field, etc.).

	Important	Unimportant
doctoral students	_____	_____
personal collections (subscriptions, papers, books, etc.)	_____	_____
university library system	_____	_____
colleagues' collections (journals, Xerox copies, books, etc.)	_____	_____
papers at professional meetings	_____	_____
departmental reading rooms (not part of the university library system)	_____	_____
conversation with colleagues on campus	_____	_____
conversation with colleagues off campus	_____	_____
other (please specify) _____	_____	_____

12. Will you please rank the sources you use in order of their importance? (Rank only sources noted as important.)

13. When did you receive your last earned degree?

> _____ 0-5 years   _____ 11-15 years
> _____ 6-10 years   _____ 16-20 years

14a. Are you currently working on another degree?
    _____ yes   _____ no

14b. If yes, in what area? _____ Degree _____

15. What is your reaction to the following statement: faculty ought to be able to request materials from a library and have them delivered to his office.
    _____ strongly agree   _____ disagree
    _____ agree   _____ strongly disagree
    _____ uncertain
    Why?

16. What is your reaction to the following statement: graduate students should be able to request materials from a library and have them delivered to their offices?
    _____ strongly agree   _____ disagree
    _____ agree   _____ strongly disagree
    _____ uncertain
    Why?

17. We would appreciate having copies of reading lists for your courses and a list of your recent publications.
    _____ received list of publications
    _____ received reading list

18. We have you listed as teaching or as having taught the following courses this year. Is our list correct? (Add any not listed.)

    _____
    _____
    _____

    _____ yes   _____ no

19. What are your current research interests? Do they differ from your teaching or past research concerns?

    _____
    _____
    _____

    _____ yes   _____ no

20. If the respondent signals out doctoral students as being important sources, ask him to identify those students who provide him with information.

    _____
    _____

Appendix A-3

TABULATIONS FOR SU INTERVIEWS

Department	f		f
Air Force, ROTC	2	Library Science	1
Anthropology	3	Management	5
Architecture	3	Mathematics	1
Army, ROTC	1	Philosophy	2
Biology	2	Physics	1
Chemistry	4	Political Science	3
Economics	3	Psychology	4
Education	7	Public Communications	2
Engineering	9	Religion	2
English	4	Romance Languages	1
Fine Arts	2	Science Teaching	1
Geography	3	Social Work	6
German	1	Sociology	1
History	7	Visual & Performing Arts	13
Human Development	6		100

Rank	f	Degree	f
Full professor	23	Doctorate	59
Associate professor	22	Master	34
Assistant professor	40	Bachelor	7
Instructor	6		100
Lecturer	9		
	100		

Branch Library	f
Branch same building as office	14
Branch not same building as office	38
Total with branch	52
Total without branch	48

1. Do you usually go to the library yourself to get a specific item?

Yes	89
No	11
	100

2. Do you ever send anyone else to the library to get a specific item?

Yes	50
No	48
No answer	2
	100

3a. Who goes to the library?

Himself only	46
Himself + someone	43
Does not go nor send	4
Sends only	7
	100

	f
Himself only	46
Himself + research assistant	6
Himself + graduate assistant	18
Himself + undergraduate	3
Himself + other	3
Himself + grad asst + undergrad	7
Himself + grad asst + other	1
Himself + secretary + res. asst	2
Himself + sec. + grad asst + undergrad	1
Himself + res asst + undergrad	1
Himself + secretary + undergrad	1
Sends research assistant	2
Sends graduate assistant	2
Sends other	1
Sends grad asst + undergrad	2
Does not go nor send	4
	100

3b. When you send, whom do you send?

Secretary	4
Research assistant	11
Graduate assistant	31
Student employee	0
Undergraduate	15
Others	5

Appendices

4. Which libraries on campus do you use?

	f
Carnegie	75
Music	10
Art, Architecture, Human Development	26
Chemistry	9
Citizenship	21
Engineering	14
Journalism	6
Law	4
Mathematics	11
Natural Science	18
Physics	10
Social Work	10
University College	2
Others*	18
No library	4

*Others--Libraries that are not part of University Library System (Upstate, Forestry, Film Library, Slide Room, Continuing Education, Special Collections--Arents, Mayfield, & Manuscript Annex) or that house materials which are not classified by LC and included in the university shelf list.

Number of Libraries Used by Respondents, Grouped by Department

| Department | No Library | Number Library Used | | | | | Total |
		1	2	3	4	5	6	
Biology		1		1				2
Chemistry		1		2		1		4
Economics			1		2			3
Engineering			2	2	2	2	1	9
Geography			1	1	1			3
Mathematics		1						1
Physics			1					1
Psychology		1	3					4
Science Teaching		1						1
Air Force, ROTC	1	1						2
Army, ROTC		1						1
Architecture				1	1		1	3
Education	1	4	2					7
Human Development			2	1	2	1		6

4 (cont).

Department	No Library	Number Library Used 1 2 3 4 5 6						Total
Management	1	1		2	1			5
Library Science			1					1
Public Communications			1	1				2
Visual & Performing Arts		5	5	2	1			13
Social Work			1	4	1			6
Anthropology		1	1	1				3
English	1	3						4
Fine Arts			1	1				2
German			1					1
History			4	1		2		7
Philosophy		1	1					2
Political Science		1	1	1				3
Religion			1		1			2
Romance Languages		1						1
Sociology					1			1

Percent of Holdings with Rank of Library Used (Data from #4 with Document Dispersion Patterns)

Percent Holdings	Rank of Libraries Used					
	1st	2nd*	3rd	4th	5th	6th
0-ns	1	9	7	4	2	1
1-10	6	26	14	10	5	1
11-20	7	4	8	1		
21-30	3	6	2	1		
31-40	5	3	1			
41-50	2	1	1			
51-60	9	3				
61-70	7	2		1		
71-80	8	6				
81-90	13	2	2			
91-100	29	3				
Other library	6	6	5	1		
Total	96	71	40	18	7	2
No Library	4					
	100					

*Note: Large number between 0-10% in second place ranking is of little significance because many 1st ranked libraries held 90-100% of an individual's relevant materials.

Appendices

Cross Tabulation: Library Usage with Document Holdings
(Data from #4 with Document Dispersion Patterns)

First used library = highest % of holdings	69
First used library ≠ highest % of holdings	20
Tie with other library for highest	1
No library	4
First choice library not part of university library system	6
	100

5. Would you rank the libraries in order of the frequency in which you use them?

Library	Total Use	Use by Library Ranking					
		1	2	3	4	5	6
Carnegie	75	41	21	7	3	3	-
Music	10	7	3	-	-	-	-
Art, Architecture, Human Development	26	10	9	7	-	-	-
Chemistry	9	4	1	3	1	-	-
Maxwell	21	3	11	5	2	-	-
Engineering	14	8	2	1	2	1	-
Journalism	6	1	-	1	3	1	-
Law	4	1	2	1	-	-	-
Mathematics	11	2	5	2	-	1	1
Natural Science	18	6	4	5	2	1	-
Physics	10	1	6	2	1	-	-
Social Work	10	6	-	-	3	-	1
University College	2	-	1	1	-	-	-
Others	18	6	6	5	1	-	-
Totals		96	71	40	18	7	2
No library		4					

6a. Do you have a reading room?
   Yes   49
   No   50
   No answer   1
                100

6b. Where is it located?
   With only three exceptions, the reading rooms were situated in respondents' office buildings.

7. If yes, do you use the departmental reading room yourself or give students assignments in materials stacked there?

	f	%
Uses himself	15	31
Gives assignments	7	14
Uses himself & gives assignments	14	29
Does not use at all	13	26
	49	100

Summary:		f	%
	Uses himself	29	59
	Gives assignments	21	43
	Does not use	13	26
		49	129*

*More than 100% because many respondents gave more than one answer.

Selected Comments:
Do use reading room:

"I use it myself and leave assignments there. Many of us shelve some of our own materials in the reading room, but we keep the collection small because of the danger of theft."

"I use it myself. There are a few reference tools in the room that I like. I am strongly in favor of reading rooms."

"I use the reading room and leave assignments there. It's the only source of materials and copies of articles related to my program of instruction."

"I read journals in the reading room."

"I use it especially for reference materials and data tables. It's strictly for research."

"I use it myself. The department subscribes to some journals."

"I give assignments. My students are required to use the census materials which are stored there."

"I used to reserve materials at Carnegie, but now I use our reading room. I found that students do use the reading room but did not use Carnegie very much."

Appendices

"I use the reading room whenever possible. The hike to the library is very inconvenient and time consuming."

"I leave books in the reading room for student assignments."

"I use the departmental reading room only occasionally. It is easier to go to the Medical Center Library."

"I give listening assignments for my conducting class there. There is no time to cover every composition in class so students must listen to specific selections in the reading room and interpret them for conducting purposes. We have been trying for years to have a branch library at Crouse College rather than at Carnegie."

<u>Do not use reading room:</u>

"I rarely use the reading room myself. My courses are organized into self-instructional units, and I keep a file of readings in my lab."

"I do not use the reading room for myself or for student assignments. I xerox copies of important materials and give them to my students."

"I do not use the reading room. All it is is some old books or duplicate copies that different faculty members want to get rid of."

"No, the department does not have a reading room. We have decided to build up our own collections conscientiously and have agreed to borrow among ourselves."

8a. When you need a specific item from the library, what would you estimate as your expectation that when you leave the library, you will have that item in hand? (scale: 0-10)

8a (cont).

ER*	f	ER*	f
0.0	3	5.5	3
0.5	0	6.0	9
1.0	3	6.5	4
1.5	0	7.0	9
2.0	3	7.5	7
2.5	1	8.0	12
3.0	2	8.5	1
3.5	3	9.0	7
4.0	3	9.5	1
4.5	1	10.0	2
5.0	23	N.A.	3
			100

$\bar{X}$ ER = 5.76
*If subject gave more than one ER, his ER equaled the average of all ERs given.

8b. to 8g. Persons sent to library by respondent and his expectation rate.

Person Sent	Number	Expectation Rate		
		The Same	Higher	Lower
Secretary	4	3	1	
Graduate assistant	31	19	9	3
Research assistant	11	6	4	1
Undergraduate	15	8	3	4
Others	5	2	3	
Total	66	38	20	8

Selected Comments*

"I know the journals that are there. It is highly probable that my requests will be successful."

---

*Note that most respondents in commenting upon their given expectation rate were citing specific parts of the library system--central library vs a branch or were making comparison of specific types of materials--journal articles, new books, microfilm, slides, etc. The positive impact of a helpful librarian, particularly in the smaller branch libraries, was impossible to ignore.

Appendices

"I have only been disappointed one or two times with our branch library. That's a good record in six years."

"We have a very good librarian in our branch. She makes sure that things are there. When I first came three years ago, it was not as good. If things are not there, it's upsetting, but she usually sends to another institution for it."

"It depends upon what I'm looking for. Usually, I can find journal articles."

"I don't like the restrictions on circulation of materials. Although I have long articles that I need to study, I'm not allowed to check them out. The annex storage is very inconvenient. I don't like to have to wait three or four hours for a reference source."

"I feel the collection in my interest area is very minimal, especially in microfilms. I do get a lot of help from our branch librarian who helps me find out where to get what I need."

"Usually I order things through my branch librarian. I just wait for them to come. But so many books are just not available even when they are listed in the card catalog."

"I look for things in my area among my colleagues' collections. I guess my feeling about the library is inevitable. It's a common one. It is just harder to look for something than it ought to be."

"I rarely use the library. It just doesn't have what I want. The popular titles are impossible to get. I have everything in my own library or in the departmental library."

"For the most part, the books that are listed in the card catalog are not to be found. They are not on the shelf. Most of my trips to the library are in vain."

"The books are stolen or mislaid. The students may be at fault. Many times whole articles are missing from the journals."

"I feel that the library is inadequate for a wide range of research. It's probably because of its inability to control its resources. Even when it's supposed to have something, you can't get your hands on it."

"I ask our librarian (research center's staff) to get it and she does. Always very fast."

Cross Tabulation: #8 with #4.

Expectation Rate and First Used Library (Carnegie or Branch)

Expectation Rate	First Used Library Carnegie	Branch
0.0	-	1
0.5	-	-
1.0	2	-
1.5	-	-
2.0	2	-
2.5	-	-
3.0	2	-
3.5	3	-
4.0	1	1
4.5	-	-
5.0	15	7
5.5	2	1
6.0	3	6
6.5	1	3
7.0	2	7
7.5	1	5
8.0	4	8
8.5	1	-
9.0	-	7
9.5	-	1
10.0	-	2
No ER	2	-
Total	41	49
Mean ER	5.1	7.0

Appendices

Cross Tabulation: #8 and heading data.

Expectation Rate With Availability of Branch and its Location

Category	No.	Mean ER
Branch same building as office	14	7.39
Branch not same building as office	38	6.58
No branch	48	4.88
	100	

Cross Tabulation: #8 and heading data.

Rank	No.	Mean ER	Remarks
Full professor	22	6.7	
Associate professor	22	6.5	1 respondent had no ER
Assistant professor	40	5.5	3 respondents had no ER
Instructor	7	6.0	
Lecturer	9	4.2	

9. When you last tried to find a specific item, were you satisfied or dissatisfied with the results? (Includes cross tabulation with #8).

	No.	Mean ER
Satisfied	59	7.0
Dissatisfied	38	4.3
Don't remember	1	5.0
No answer	2	-
	100	

10. Do you organize your courses to include student use of the library system?

Yes	63
No	37
	100

Selected Comments:

Yes - do organize courses for library use.

"My courses involve a lot of papers. Students need to read journal articles. At the undergraduate level, I use reserve reading lists; at the graduate level, I expect them to use primary sources. They have to dig for them!"

"I issue reading lists for each course."

"For some courses, yes, and for some, no. It depends upon the nature of the course. Special research projects require information from library sources; and occasionally, I use the reserve shelf."

"I do have a bibliography available for my students, but I do not assign specific readings. I hope they do them."

"I did in the fall but not in the spring semester. I have decided that the text is sufficient. I used to reserve but it was too restrictive. I wanted the students to have the books longer. Also, the library doesn't have everything that I want. Now I loan my personal books to students."

"I put books on reserve and assign papers. Actually, there are a lot of paperback possibilities so students can purchase much of the materials they need for my courses. I do not trust the library."

"Primary source materials are used for a lot of my course work. I also use the reserve book room and assign research papers which require the use of the library."

"I place books on reserve and assign papers. I also throw out suggestions of specific books and periodical articles in my lectures."

"Graduate level courses involve the reading of a good deal of the current literature in the field--journal articles and so forth."

"I have reading lists and research papers and use microfiche collection for primary source material."

"I expect graduate students to use the library. With undergraduates, no. They don't have to. Their texts are enough."

Appendices   105

"I use reserve books. Graduate students will buy a
few things for themselves, but most of them depend
upon my personal collection. I have to put a lot of
my own materials on reserve. I also use paperbacks
for a wide exposure to the ideas I want to cover.
Some of the students buy them."

"I have bibliographies for specific topics covered in
the syllabus. I also depend heavily on periodicals
outside of my own discipline. Much of what I need is
very current--information from newspapers and bookstores. I can't wait for the library to get it, so I
keep up with the newsstands, bookstores and whatever
is new."

"Library use is stressed, but there are no required
readings."

"I try to emphasize library use. I give out a library
manual to all my students which is revised every two
years after consulting with the branch librarian for any
additions or changes in his organization of the books,
etc."

<u>No</u> - do not organize courses to include library work.

"No, not for undergraduate courses."

"I do not orient my course assignments around the library resources because it is such an uncomfortable
facility, and students are wary of using it. Also the
materials that I am interested in using are available
in paperback editions. I do put things on reserve if
the students don't want to buy them. I could use the
library for an outside reading room. Graduate students do have research projects, and they must use
the library for some of their work."

"No, my personal collection is the source of all my
class readings."

"My course work includes very little use of the library. I try, instead, to put as much information as
possible in handout form. I try to weed out information for the students so that they only spend their
time on what's important. Then students can do more

independent learning on specific topics for projects that they are interested in."

"No, not directly. I do have recommended reading lists that I give to both the students and the librarians. But it is only supplementary reading. I rely primarily on the text. Occasionally, I give research projects and then the students need the library."

"I try to avoid it by using paperbacks."

"I have a large introductory course and it is hopeless to assign readings and expect students to be able to come up with specific titles. There are not enough books to go around. For other courses and students who are working in a specialized area, I loan my own copies to them. So many of the materials tend to be out of date in a few years, anyway."

"I Xerox journal articles and put them on reserve sometimes. My assignments do not involve the use of other library materials. I tend to use popular magazines for undergraduate courses because they are more readily available to students at home or on the newsstands."

"I recommend paperbacks to avoid the library. There are a few instances where the student must go to the library, but I encourage them to purchase their own."

"Occasionally, I require the students to look at the 'Little Magazines' located in the periodical room. Whenever possible, though, I use my own personal collection for source materials for courses."

"Rarely, I depend upon texts. I want my students to own their own readings. I do hope that the new library has larger reading rooms."

"I try to organize my course so that they do not use the library. I teach statistics and use texts primarily. There really is no need for assigned readings. I really do not require a library in the traditional sense, but I do need a computing library, and I use the computer center references frequently."

"It's not built in to the course but it should be. I do have assignments where they should use the library, but it's not an integral part of the course. For one of my large classes, the library just cannot cope with all the students. I make tapes and slides on various units and labs. Then the students have a room equipped with projectors, recorders and microscopes for individualized study of the materials covered in the course. I try to avoid the library. It doesn't have what I need at my level. It's too hard to find anything. I rely on my own sources."

Summary of Comments: Types of Library Use in Support of Courses

Type of Use	f
Reserved reading	42
Term papers (research papers)	30
Use of special forms of materials as part of project or background reading:	
(1) journals	11
(2) phonorecords	4
(3) scores	3
(4) microfilms	1
(5) reference books	3
Supplementary readings listed in class reading lists, course syllabi or suggested in lectures:	
(1) reading lists, syllabi, bibliographies	15
(2) lectures	13

11. Which of the following sources do you consider important for your teaching and research needs?

	Important	Unimportant
Doctoral students	49	51
Personal collections	96	4
University library system	78	22
Colleagues' collection	50	50
Papers at meetings	50	50
Dept'l reading room*	19	30
Conversation--on campus	75	25
Conversation--off campus	74	26
Others	24	

*Only 49 respondents had departmental reading rooms.

12. Rank the sources which are important to you in order of their importance.

Source	% Rank Impt.	X̄ Ranking	% 1st	% 2nd	% 3rd	% 4th	% 5th	% 6th	% 7th
Personal collections	96	1.59	60	21	10	4	1		
University library system	78	2.70	23	23	12	7	5	3	5
Others	24	3.42	5	2	7	2	4	4	
Departmental reading room	19	3.52	2	4	3	6	2		2
Conversation--on campus	75	3.65	4	15	13	20	18	4	1
Papers at meetings	50	3.98	3	9	10	6	11	8	3
Conversation--off campus	74	4.01	2	10	17	20	11	9	5
Colleagues' collection	50	4.06	4	7	8	9	10	9	3
Doctoral students	49	4.14	3	8	7	9	8	11	3

Cross Tabulation: #11 with #8.

Importance of Library as Information Source and Mean Expectation Rate

	No.	Mean ER
Important	78	6.18
Unimportant	22	4.77
	100	

Cross Tabulation: #11 with #10.

Use of Library for Class Work and Importance of Library

	Library Important		Library Unimportant	
	n	%	n	%
Use library for class	57	73	6	27
Not use library	21	27	16	73
	78	100	22	100

Appendices

Cross Tabulation: #11 with #12 with heading data.

Faculty Rank and Library System Considered Important-Unimportant Source

Faculty Rank	Number	Unimportant n	%	Important n	%	X̄ ranking for library
Full professor	23	2	9	21	91	2.86
Associate professor	22	4	18	18	82	2.71
Assistant professor	39	9	23	30	77	2.76
Instructor	7	2	26	5	71	2.20
Lecturer	9	5	56	4	44	2.25
Total	100	22		78		

13. When did you receive your last earned degree?

Years Since Last Degree	n
0 to 5 years	39
6 to 10 years	26
11 to 15 years	9
16 to 20 years	10
More than 20 years	16
	100

Cross Tabulation: #13 with #11 and #12.

Years Since Last Degree & Importance of Library as Source of Information

Category	Important n	X̄ ranking	Unimportant n	Total
0 to 5 years	28	2.68	11	39
6 to 10 years	21	2.57	5	26
11 to 15 years	8	2.75	1	9
16 to 20 years	7	2.86	3	10
More than 20 years	14	2.93	2	16
Total	78		22	100

14a. Are you currently working on another degree?

           Yes   20
           No   80
                 ———
                 100

Cross Tabulation: #14 with #11.

Working on a Degree and Importance of Library as Source of Information

Category	Important n $\bar{X}$ ranking		Unimportant n	Total
Working on degree	15	2.47	5	20
Not working on degree	63	2.78	17	80

14b. In what area are you working for a degree?
     Not tabulated. Classifiers used the information to complete interest profile for each individual.

#15 and #16. Reaction to delivery service: Faculty-graduate students ought to be able to request materials from a library and have them delivered.

	Faculty	Students
Strongly agree	15	1
Agree	32	14
Uncertain	11	16
Disagree	36	43
Strongly disagree	6	26
	100	100

Cross Tabulation of #15 and #16 with heading data: Attitudes toward delivery with branch library vs no branch.

	Branch	No Branch
S.A.	9	6
A.	15	17
U.	7	2
D.	17	21
S.D.	4	2
	52	48

Appendices

Cross Tabulation: #15 with #11.

Delivery for Faculty Attitude	Last Use of Library			
	Satisfied		Dissatisfied	
	n	%	n	%
Strongly agree	8	14	7	18
Agree	18	30	12	32
Uncertain	7	12	4	10
Disagree	23	39	12	32
Strongly disagree	3	5	3	8
	59*		38*	

*Total = 97 because 3 respondents did not answer satisfied-dissatisfied question.

Summary of Comments: Faculty should be able to request materials and have them delivered.

Agree:
1. time saver
2. parking problem
3. holdings on campus dispersed
4. saves money
5. convenience
6. reduce discouragement and frustration. Let library staff experience the frustration.
7. will be able to spend more time teaching and counseling.

Disagree:
1. should use the library themselves
2. wish to retain browsing
3. no reason
4. too time consuming for library personnel
5. poor use of library funds
6. students can be used to fetch materials
7. useless waste of resources
8. materials would not be returned to the library
9. financially impossible
10. not essential to the researcher
11. faculty are not that busy
12. library can go too far in providing services
13. already have access to a branch library

Summary of Comments: Graduate students should be able to request materials and have them delivered.

<u>Agree:</u>
1. time saver
2. will reduce book losses

<u>Disagree:</u>
1. not economical
2. library use is an integral part of a graduate student's experience
3. too many students
4. need to become familiar with resources in his discipline
5. should be forced to browse

Selected Comments: Delivery Service for Faculty

<u>Strongly agree:</u>

"Yes, a good idea for someone who doesn't have a library nearby. It's time consuming to make trips back and forth. Then you have to spend several hours looking for what you want."

"Speed, time, efficiency and convenience. I don't always get there when I should, especially when the distance between my office and the branch I want to go to increases. Then I have trouble retrieving materials."

"I agree in principle, but would have reservations if the service diverted funds from more important things, e.g., salaries."

"A magnificent idea! What a time saver! I don't know if it's financially possible, but it would be nice to get things with just a phone call."

"Access to the library is bad because the campus is so decentralized. Parking is impossible."

<u>Agree:</u>

"Faculty carrying special responsibilities in addition to their regular loads ought to be given this service. Others should use the library themselves."

> "My time is limited. I have limited use of graduate students and secretarial help. It would be a tremendous help if the library would do the searching for me. I wouldn't mind going over to pick things up, if I knew that they would be waiting for me when I got there."
>
> "Such a service would provide support to the faculty. It would enable them to be more productive."

Uncertain:

> "Ask me next year (library right outside office door). If library is not as convenient when they move to 'Bird,' I may think it very important. Of course, there is the question of cost."

Disagree:

> "It would be nice but should spend library funds on other more important things. Students can be used to fetch."
>
> "A useless waste of resources."
>
> "A costly endeavor and it's not essential to researcher. I like to browse among the stacks. I wouldn't want to give up this activity."
>
> "Faculty are not that busy."
>
> "I would like to request books and have them gathered for me. I would be willing to pick them up."
>
> "It might be OK if libraries are far distant from the faculty's office."

Strongly Disagree:

> "Library has other jobs to do. Shouldn't spend time and money on a messenger service. Should spend time on improving services."
>
> "I'm not lazy."

"It would encourage laziness. It adds to unnecessary expense. Faculty members should get to know the library system themselves. It's like faculty members not running film projectors themselves. Have to spend the money for an AV center aide. A total waste."

"That's not a library function. It would take vital resources that could be spent in acquiring materials and putting them into service. It's just a wrong allocation of resources. They should spend their time and money teaching students how to use the library."

Selected Comments: Delivery Service for Students

Agree:

"Some students have the time to go to the library. Some students on assistantships don't have the time. They should have the service."

"Not for any graduate student. They need the library experience. Just for those who are functioning as staff members."

"It saves time. I am assuming that they know how to use the library. If they don't know, they should learn how to find materials for themselves. Doing it is the only way to learn."

Uncertain:

"I feel seminar library rooms are more important. They need rooms where they can work and have texts, readings and other materials for their coursework and research readily available to them."

Disagree and strongly disagree:

"It would be economically unfeasible. In our department, we have a 6:1 ratio of students to faculty."

"Library experience is good for them and they are negligent about returning materials."

"They should be familiar with the library resources and library use is part of their professional growth."

"Using the library is a learning experience for the student."

"Funds are better spent on building up the collection."

"We have money problems as it is. Delivery service to students should have a very low priority."

"They should be forced to browse."

"They learn by using the library. The library opens many doors in research. Intelligent use of the library a must."

17 and 18. Not tabulated. Classifiers used data to construct interest profile for each individual.

19. Do your current research interests differ from your teaching or past research concerns?

    Yes   59
    No   33
    No answer   8
               ___
               100

20. The names of doctoral students were listed as possible subjects for another study.

Appendix B-1

INSTRUCTIONS FOR SHELF LIST COUNT OF DOCUMENT DISPERSION PATTERNS AT THE LIBRARY PROCESSING CENTER

A. Total count of titles in class no.
1. if long run--measure in inches. Measure 1 inch of cards held firmly between fingers (but not squeezed). Count 87 cards per inch; 44 cards per half inch; and 21 cards per 1/4 inch.
2. if short run in class no.--count cards. If one title has more than one card, count only once.
3. only interested in no. of titles--not in no. of volumes or copies.
4. if serial title changes, count old and new title as one title.
5. because of multiple copies, you should expect to have more titles in different locations than your total count indicates.
6. if total count is more than location count, probably means there were several serials in shelf list with more than 1 card/title. Check to validate such cards. If few serials, recount. If several, we will adjust it for you.

B. Location of titles in class no.
1. must go through card by card and check off location of each copy.
2. if more than 1 copy in the same location--count only once.
3. if same title is in more than one location, check off each location except,
   (a) Do put title in every branch he does use, if title is in more than one branch he uses.
   (b) Do put title in branches he doesn't use, if not in branches he does use.
   (c) Do not put a title with more than 1 copy in branches respondent does not use, if it is in one or more of the branches he does use.

Appendices

4. be sure to list libraries in same order in successive work sheets as in first work sheet for a specific respondent.
5. Abbreviations and other notations:
   (a) SV = Social Work branch
   (b) 4W = Social Work branch
   (c) EH = Human Development--locate with Art, Architecture, etc.
6. because each subject's library use pattern differs, locations for same LC number must be tabulated for each individual.

C. Notes in SU shelf list arrangement
   serial titles are included in main shelf list without a location notation.
   (a) count as title in main shelf list with other monographs.
   (b) must go to serials shelf list for location.

D. Serials shelf list file
   1. has two or more cards for each serial title
      Card #1--main entry card
      Card #2,3, ... holdings card and must include location
   2. Holding card
      if serial shelved in more than one location, there will be a "holding card" for each separate location, giving both the branch and what volumes are shelved there. Follow rules in B above for noting location of serials.

DOCUMENT DISPERSION PATTERN   B - 2

WORKSHEET

Call No.	Physics	Mathematics	Engineering	Carnegie	Chemistry	Univ. College	Nat'l Science
QC 1	#### #### #### #### #### #### #### ####	////	#### ///	////	####		
QC 173	#### #### #### #### #### #### #### #### #### ////	/	#### #### ####	#### #### /	#### #### #### //	/	//
QC 415	####		/		//		/
QC 447	#### ////		///				
QC 481-2	#### ///		#### ////	/	#### #### ####		////
QC 721	#### #### #### #### #### #### #### #### #### #### ####	#### #### ///	#### #### ####	####	#### ///		

Appendices

Worksheet (continued)

Call No.	Physics	Mathematics	Engineering	Carnegie	Chemistry	Univ. College	Nat'l Science
QC 721 (con't)	‖‖‖ ‖‖‖ ‖‖‖ ‖‖‖ ////						
QC 757	‖‖‖ //		///				
QD 901	//		//		‖‖‖ //	/	/
QD 921	‖‖‖ ‖‖‖ ‖‖‖ //		‖‖‖ /		‖‖‖ ‖‖‖ // ‖‖‖ ‖‖‖ /		//
QD 931-41	‖‖‖ ‖‖‖ ‖‖‖ ‖‖‖ //		‖‖‖ ////	/	‖‖‖ ‖‖‖ ‖‖‖		///
QD 945	‖‖‖ ‖‖‖ ‖‖‖ ‖‖‖ ////	/	‖‖‖ ‖‖‖ ‖‖‖ ‖‖‖	/	‖‖‖ ‖‖‖ ‖‖‖ ‖‖‖ ////		
QH 201-19	‖‖‖ ‖‖‖		‖‖‖ //	/	////		
T 1	‖‖‖ //		‖‖‖ ‖‖‖ // ‖‖‖ ‖‖‖ // ‖‖‖ ‖‖‖ / ‖‖‖ ‖‖‖ ‖‖‖ ‖‖‖ ‖‖‖ ‖‖‖	‖‖‖ ‖‖‖ ‖‖‖ ‖‖‖			‖‖‖ ‖‖‖ ‖‖‖ ‖‖‖ ‖‖‖ ‖‖‖
TA 418.5	///		‖‖‖ ‖‖‖ //		///		
TJ 940	‖‖‖ ‖‖‖ //		‖‖‖ //	‖‖‖ //	‖‖‖ ‖‖‖ ///		‖‖‖ ‖‖‖
TN 1	/		‖‖‖ ‖‖‖ // ‖‖‖ ////		‖‖‖ ‖‖‖ ///		
TN 690	////		‖‖‖ ‖‖‖ // ‖‖‖ ‖‖‖ // ‖‖‖ ‖‖‖ / ‖‖‖ ‖‖‖	/	‖‖‖ ‖‖‖ ‖‖‖ // ‖‖‖ ‖‖‖ /		
Totals	535 (47%)	25 (2%)	266 (24%)	52 (5%)	178 (16%)	1 (ns)	64 (6%)

Appendix B-3

SHELF LIST COUNT OF
DOCUMENT DISPERSION PATTERNS--EXPLANATION

The document dispersion patterns for the one hundred Syracuse University faculty interviewed are found in Appendix B-4. The code below explains the abbreviations used for the various libraries which faculty reportedly frequented in search of information.

Code for Libraries Included in the
Document Dispersion Patterns

AAHD	Art, Architecture, Human Development Library	Law	Law Library
		Mat	Mathematics Library
		Med*	Upstate Medical Center Library
Cen	Central or Main Library	Mus	Music Library
Che	Chemistry Library	NSc	Natural Science Library
Cit	Citizenship Library		
CEd*	Continuing Education Library	Phy	Physics Library
		Sli*	Slide Room
Eng	Engineering Library	SoW	Social Work Library
Fil*	Film Library	UnC	University College Library
For*	Forestry Library		
Jou	Journalism Library		

*Libraries which are not part of the University Library system or which house specialized materials which are not fully classified by Library of Congress Classification system and are not included in the SU shelf list.

The pattern for each individual relates his library usage with both the location and percent of holdings of potentially relevant materials in the total library system. It also indicates his document exposure index (DEI) and the rank order of distance from an individual's office to the various libraries which he reportedly used.

Appendices

For example, the biologist, #123 (See Appendix B-4), claimed to use three libraries: Natural Science, the central library and Chemistry. Material of potential relevance to his information needs was dispersed throughout seven libraries in the university system. Two of the seven libraries have a non-substantial (ns) percentage of relevant materials. The library which #123 frequents most often is also the library with the highest percent of relevant holdings--70 percent; his second and third choice libraries ranked third and second respectively in terms of the percent of potentially relevant material housed therein. Apparently, he did not select his library outlets on the basis of proximity to his office, for the three libraries he reportedly frequented ranked second, third and fifth in distance from his office to the library branch.

Appendix B-4

SHELF LIST COUNT OF DOCUMENT DISPERSION PATTERNS
(Includes the document exposure index--DEI, the rank order of
libraries used, and the rank order of distances between each
library and the subject's office).

Group I - Sciences

Department	Code	Library	% of Holdings	Rank Order Holdings	Rank Order of Use	Rank Distance	DEI
Air Force	061	Cen	65	1	1	2	65
		Eng	23	2		1	
		NSc	6	3		3	
		Cit	5	4		4	
Biology	069	NSc	69	1	1	2	69
		Cen	17	2		3	
		Che	5	3		6	
		Mat	4	4		5	
		Eng	2	5		1	
		Phy	2	6		4	
	123	NSc	70	1	1	2	97
		Cen	8	3	2	3	
		Che	19	2	3	5	
		Phy	2	4		4	
		Eng	1	5		1	
		Mat	ns				
		UnC	ns				
Chemistry	020	Che	87	1	1	1	87
		NSc	4	3		5	
		Eng	4	2		2	
		AAHD	ns				
		Phy	3	4		3	
		Cen	2	5		4	
		Mat	ns				
	034	Che	37	1	1	1	77
		Phy	37	2	2	3	
		NSc	2	5	3	5	
		Med*			4		
		Cen	1	6	5	4	
		Mat	12	3		6	
		Eng	11	4		2	
		Mus	ns				

Department	Code	Library	% of Holdings	Rank Order Holdings	Rank Order of Use	Rank Distance	DEI
Chemistry	044	Che	80	1	1	1	82
		For*			2		
		Cen	2	4	3	4	
		NSc	12	2		2	
		Eng	4	3		3	
		Phy	2	5		5	
		AAHD	ns				
		Mat	ns				
	051	Che	54	1	1	1	94
		Phy	21	2	2	3	
		Eng	19	3	3	2	
		Cen	2	4		4	
		NSc	2	5		5	
		AAHD	1	6		6	
		Mat	ns				
		Mus	ns				
		Jou	ns				
		UnC	ns				
Engineering	017	Cen	60	1	1	5	81
		Eng	21	2	2	1	
		Med*			3		
		Mat	16	3		4	
		Phy	1	4		2	
		UnC	1	5		3	
		Jou	1	6		6	
	023	Eng	38	1	1	1	100
		Che	27	2	2	3	
		Cen	12	3	3	5	
		Phy	11	4	4	3	
		NSc	3	6	5	2	
		Mat	9	5	6	4	
		AAHD	ns				
		Cit	ns				
		UnC	ns				
		Jou	ns				
	024	Eng	56	1	1	1	63
		Mat	7	4	2	5	
		Cen	19	2		6	
		UnC	1	9		9	
		Jou	ns				
		Cit	3	5		7	
		Phy	1	8		3	
		NSc	3	6		2	
		AAHD	8	3		8	
		Che	1	7		4	

Department	Code	Library	% of Holdings	Rank Order Holdings	Rank Order of Use	Rank Distance	DEI
Engineering	039	Eng	46	1	1	1	61
		Phy	15	3	2	3	
		Che	28	2		2	
		Cen	6	4		5	
		Mat	1	6		4	
		NSc	3	5		2	
		Mus	ns				
		Cit	ns				
	048	Eng	24	2	1	1	92
		Phy	47	1	2	3	
		Che	16	3	3	2	
		Cen	5	5	4	5	
		NSc	6	4		2	
		Mat	2	6		4	
		AAHD	ns				
		Jou	ns				
	070	Mat	38	2	1	3	99
		Eng	53	1	2	1	
		Phy	1	4	3	2	
		NSc	ns		4		
		Cen	7	3	5	4	
		AAHD	1	5		5	
	073	Eng	9	3	1	1	98
		Phy	63	1	2	2	
		Mat	24	2	3	3	
		Cen	2	4	4	4	
		Che	1	5		5	
		NSc	ns				
		Cit	ns				
		AAHD	ns				
	075	Eng	75	1	1	1	94
		Phy	2	4	2	3	
		Che	11	2	3	8	
		Jou	0		4	5	
		Cen	6	3	5	4	
		NSc	2	5		2	
		AAHD	2	6		7	
		Mat	1	7		6	
		Cit	ns				
	094	Eng	58	1	1	1	86
		Mat	18	2	2	3	
		Phy	10	4	3	2	
		Cen	11	3		4	
		Che	1	5		6	
		AAHD	1	6		5	
		UnC	ns				
		Cit	ns				
		NSc	ns				
		Jou	ns				

Appendices   125

Department	Code	Library	% of Holdings	Rank Order Holdings	Rank Order of Use	Rank Distance	DEI
Human Development	037	AAHD	11	4	1	1	77
		Med*			2		
		NSc	43	1	3	2	
		Che	23	2	4	4	
		Cen	23	3		3	
		Eng	ns				
		Phy	ns				
Mathematics	018	Mat	86	1	1	2	86
		Eng	9	2		1	
		Phy	2	3		3	
		Cen	2	4		4	
		Che	ns				
		NSc	ns				
		UnC	ns				
Physics	122	Phy	62	1	1	1	62
		Cen	6	4	2	3	
		Che	9	3		6	
		Eng	17	2		2	
		Mat	4	5		5	
		NSc	2	6		4	
		Cit	ns				
Psychology	013	Cen	49	1	1	3	49
		Med*			2		
		Eng	19	2		1	
		Mat	16	3		5	
		Phy	9	4		4	
		NSc	4	5		2	
		Che	1	6		6	
		AAHD	ns				
		Cit	ns				
		Mus	ns				
		SoW	ns				
		UnC	ns				
		Jou	ns				
	025	Cen	96	1	1	2	96
		SoW	2	2		1	
		AAHD	1	3		3	
		UnC	ns				
		Eng	ns				
		Mat	ns				
		Jou	ns				
		NSc	ns				
		Cit	ns				

Department	Code	Library	% of Holdings	Rank Order Holdings	Rank Order of Use	Rank Distance	DEI
Psychology	026	Med*			1		52
		Cen	52	1	2	5	
		Mat	34	2		4	
		Eng	7	3		1	
		Phy	2	4		2	
		UnC	2	5		7	
		Che	1	6		6	
		NSc	1	7		3	
		SoW	ns				
		AAHD	ns				
	060	Med*			1		80
		Cen	80	1	2	5	
		SoW	3	3		4	
		Mat	7	2		3	
		UnC	2	4		10	
		Eng	2	5		1	
		NSc	2	6		2	
		AAHD	1	7		8	
		Jou	1	8		6	
		Che	1	9		9	
		Phy	1	10		7	
		Cit	ns				
Science Teaching	062	NSc	60	1	1	4	60
		Cen	33	2		3	
		Phy	2	3		2	
		Che	2	4		6	
		Eng	1	5		1	
		Mat	1	6		5	
		Mus	ns				
		Cit	ns				
		AAHD	ns				
		Jou	ns				
		UnC	ns				
		SoW	ns				

Group II - Social Sciences

Department	Code	Library	% of Holdings	Rank Order Holdings	Rank Order of Use	Rank Distance	DEI
Air Force	009	Cen	70	1			0
		Eng	10	2			
		UnC	9	3			
		Cit	8	4			
		Jou	2	5			
		Mat	1	6			
		SoW	ns				
		AAHD	ns				

Department	Code	Library	% of Holdings	Rank Order Holdings	Rank Order of Use	Rank Distance	DEI
Anthropology	084	Cen	88	1	1	3	88
		NSc	ns	8	2		
		Cit	7	2		2	
		UnC	1	4		5	
		SoW	1	5		1	
		AAHD	2	3		4	
		Jou	ns				
		Law	ns				
		Eng	ns				
		Mat	ns				
	092	Cen	91	1	1	3	98
		NSc	2	3	2	2	
		AAHD	5	2	3	4	
		Cit	1	4		1	
		UnC	1	5		5	
		Law	ns				
	119	Cen	96	1	1	3	96
		Cit	1	2		2	
		Jou	1	3		1	
		UnC	1	4		4	
		NSc	ns				
		AAHD	ns				
		Eng	ns				
		SoW	ns				
		Mat	ns				
Army, ROTC	121	Law	0		1	5	0
		Cen	70	1		2	
		Eng	10	2		1	
		UnC	10	3		6	
		Cit	8	4		4	
		Jou	1	5		3	
		Mat	ns				
		AAHD	ns				
Economics	050	Cit	22	2	1	3	93
		Cen	70	1	2	5	
		NSc	ns		3		
		SoW	1	4	4	1	
		AAHD	3	3		6	
		Eng	1	5		2	
		UnC	1	6		7	
		Law	1	7		4	
		Mat	ns				
		Jou	ns				

Department	Code	Library	% of Holdings	Rank Order Holdings	Rank Order of Use	Rank Distance	DEI
Economics	090	Cen	71	1	1	3	96
		Cit	25	2	2	1	
		SoW	2	3		2	
		UnC	1	4		4	
		AAHD	1	5		5	
		Eng	ns				
		Jou	ns				
		Mus	ns				
		Law	ns				
	115	Cen	85	1	1	5	96
		Mat	5	3	2	4	
		AAHD	ns		3		
		Cit	6	2	4	2	
		UnC	1	4		6	
		Eng	1	5		3	
		SoW	1	6		1	
		Jou	ns				
		Phy	ns				
Education	010	Cen	87	1			0
		Cit	5	2			
		Jou	4	3			
		AAHD	2	4			
		UnC	1	5			
		Eng	ns				
		SoW	ns				
		Mus	ns				
	021	Cen	89	1	1	4	89
		SoW	4	2		2	
		Cit	3	3		3	
		AAHD	2	4		5	
		Jou	1	5		1	
		UnC	1	6		6	
		NSc	ns				
		Law	ns				
	038	Cen	97	1	1	1	97
		UnC	1	2		3	
		Cit	1	3		2	
		Jou	ns				
		SoW	ns				
		Mus	ns				
		AAHD	ns				

Appendices

Department	Code	Library	% of Holdings	Rank Order Holdings	Rank Order of Use	Rank Distance	DEI
Education	040	NSc	10	3	1	1	10
		Phy	1	8		3	
		Cit	6	5		6	
		Cen	56	1		4	
		AAHD	1	9		7	
		Che	13	2		8	
		Eng	8	4		2	
		Mat	ns	10			
		UnC	3	6		9	
		Jou	1	7		6	
	054	Cen	95	1	1	2	95
		Med*			2		
		Jou	2	2		1	
		UnC	2	3		3	
		Cit	ns				
		AAHD	ns				
		SoW	ns				
		Mat	ns				
		Eng	ns				
		NSc	ns				
	057	Cen	95	1	1	1	95
		CEd*			2		
		UnC	4	2		2	
		Cit	ns				
		Mus	ns				
		Eng	ns				
		Jou	ns				
		SoW	ns				
		AAHD	ns				
	058	Cen	99	1	1	1	99
		CEd*			2		
		UnC	ns				
		Jou	ns				
		Mus	ns				
Geography	029	NSc	14	2	1	2	93
		Cen	72	1	2	4	
		Cit	7	3	3	3	
		UnC	2	4		6	
		AAHD	1	7		5	
		Eng	2	5		1	
		Mat	1	6		3	
		SoW	ns				
		Che	ns				
		Phy	ns				
		Jou	ns				
		Law	ns				

130   Improving Access

Department	Code	Library	% of Holdings	Rank Order Holdings	Rank Order of Use	Rank Distance	DEI
Geography	071	NSc	20	2	1	1	100
		Cen	74	1	2	3	
		AAHD	2	4	3	4	
		Cit	4	3	4	2	
		Phy	ns				
		UnC	ns				
		Mat	ns				
		Law	ns				
	080	Cen	88	1	1	5	92
		NSc	4	2	2	2	
		Cit	2	3		4	
		Jou	2	4		1	
		Mus	ns				
		AAHD	1	5		6	
		UnC	1	6		7	
		SoW	1	7		3	
		Eng	ns				
History	008	Cen	85	1	1	5	96
		Cit	5	2	2	3	
		AAHD	3	3	3	6	
		NSc	1	6	4	4	
		Jou	2	4	5	2	
		UnC	2	5		7	
		SoW	1	7		1	
		Law	ns				
	045	Cen	75	1	1	3	96
		Cit	21	2	2	1	
		Jou	2	3		2	
		UnC	1	4		4	
		AAHD	ns				
	072	Cen	90	1	1	2	97
		AAHD	7	2	2	3	
		Cit	1	3		1	
		UnC	1	4		4	
		Mus	ns				
		Mat	ns				
		SoW	ns				
		Law	ns				
		NSc	ns				
		Eng	ns				
	097	Cen	79	1	1	5	91
		AAHD	8	2	2	6	
		Med*			3		
		SoW	4	3	4	2	
		Eng	ns		5		
		UnC	4	4		7	
		Cit	3	5		4	
		Jou	1	6		1	
		Law	1	7		3	

Appendices

Department	Code	Library	% of Holdings	Rank Order Holdings	Rank Order of Use	Rank Distance	DEI
History	110	Cen	72	1	1	5	86
		Cit	14	2	2	1	
		UnC	6	3		6	
		Jou	4	4		3	
		SoW	2	5		4	
		Mus	1	6		2	
		AAHD	ns				
		Law	ns				
	116	Cen	96	1	1	2	97
		Cit	1	3	2	1	
		UnC	2	2		3	
		Jou	ns				
		AAHD	ns				
	118	Cen	97	1	1	2	99
		Law	ns		2		
		AAHD	2	2	3	3	
		Cit	1	3		1	
		Mat	ns				
		UnC	ns				
		SoW	ns				
Human Development	053	Cen	83	1	1	4	90
		AAHD	7	2	2	3	
		SoW	7	3		1	
		UnC	2	4		5	
		NSc	1	5		2	
	091	Med*			1		96
		Cen	94	1	2	3	
		AAHD	2	2	3	4	
		UnC	1	3		5	
		Jou	1	4		2	
		SoW	1	5		1	
		Cit	ns				
		Mus	ns				
		Eng	ns				
		Mat	ns				
		NSc	ns				
	111	Med*			1		91
		AAHD	5	2	2	3	
		Cen	86	1	3	4	
		SoW	4	3		1	
		NSc	2	4		2	
		UnC	1	5		5	
		Jou	ns				
		Cit	ns				
		Phy	ns				
		Eng	ns				

Department	Code	Library	% of Holdings	Rank Order Holdings	Rank Order of Use	Rank Distance	DEI
Manage-ment	014	Cen	68	1	1	2	96
		Cit	6	3	2	5	
		Mat	16	2	3	3	
		Eng	6	4	4	1	
		UnC	2	5		6	
		AAHD	1	6		4	
		Che	ns				
		NSc	ns				
		Jou	ns				
		Phy	ns				
		SoW	ns				
	064	Cen	72	1	1	3	74
		UnC	1	5	2	6	
		NSc	1	6	3	2	
		Eng	19	2		1	
		AAHD	4	3		4	
		Cit	2	4		5	
		Law	ns				
		Jou	ns				
		SoW	ns				
		Mat	ns				
		Phy	ns				
	088	Cen	85	1			0
		Mat	3	3			
		Eng	8	2			
		UnC	2	4			
		Cit	1	5			
		AAHD	ns				
		Jou	ns				
		NSc	ns				
	113	Cen	97	1	1	1	97
		Mat	0		2		
		Law	ns		3		
		Cit	2	2		2	
		Eng	ns				
		UnC	ns				
	114	Cen	83	1	1	2	83
		Mat	6	2		3	
		Cit	4	3		4	
		Eng	4	4		1	
		UnC	2	5		5	
		AAHD	ns				
		Law	ns				
		Che	ns				
		NSc	ns				
		Phy	ns				

Appendices

Department	Code	Library	% of Holdings	Rank Order Holdings	Rank Order of Use	Rank Distance	DEI
Political Science	056	Cit	40	2	1	3	97
		Cen	55	1	2	4	
		Jou	2	3	3	2	
		UnC	2	4		5	
		SoW	1	5		1	
		Eng	ns				
		AAHD	ns				
		Law	ns				
	089	Cen	59	1	1	6	86
		Cit	27	2	2	5	
		UnC	1	5		9	
		AAHD	1	6		8	
		SoW	ns				
		Mat	4	3		4	
		Jou	1	7		1	
		Eng	3	4		3	
		Phy	1	8		7	
		NSc	1	9		2	
		Law	ns				
		Che	ns				
	105	Cit	17	2	1	1	17
		Cen	82	1		2	
		UnC	ns				
		Jou	ns				
Public Communications	001	Jou	15	2	1	1	94
		Cen	79	1	2	4	
		Cit	3	3		3	
		UnC	2	4		5	
		SoW	1	5		2	
		NSc	ns				
		AAHD	ns				
		Eng	ns				
		Law	ns				
	085	Fil*			1		87
		Mus	0		2	1	
		Cen	87	1	3	3	
		Eng	5	2		2	
		Cit	4	3		5	
		Jou	3	4		4	
		Law	1	5		3	
		AAHD	ns				
		UnC	ns				
		Mat	ns				

Department	Code	Library	% of Holdings	Rank Order Holdings	Rank Order of Use	Rank Distance	DEI
Social Work	003	SoW	8	2	1	1	98
		Cen	88	1	2	3	
		Cit	2	3	3	2	
		UnC	2	4		4	
		Eng	ns				
		NSc	ns				
		Jou	ns				
		AAHD	ns				
		Law	ns				
	007	SoW	4	2	1	1	95
		Cen	91	1	2	5	
		Med*			3		
		Jou	ns		4	2	
		UnC	1	3		7	
		AAHD	1	4		6	
		Cit	1	5		3	
		Eng	1	6		4	
		Law	ns				
		NSc	ns				
		Mat	ns				
		Mus	ns				
	035	SoW	13	2	1	1	16
		Cit	3	4	2	3	
		Med*			3		
		Cen	75	1		4	
		UnC	6	3		6	
		AAHD	2	5		5	
		Jou	1	6		2	
		NSc	ns				
		Eng	ns				
		Law	ns				
	059	SoW	20	2	1	1	89
		Law	ns		2		
		Med*			3		
		Cen	69	1	4	4	
		Jou	6	3		2	
		UnC	1	4		7	
		Cit	1	5		3	
		Che	1	6		6	
		NSc	1	7		5	
		Eng	ns				
		AAHD	ns				
	093	SoW	21	2	1	1	95
		Cen	74	1	2	3	
		UnC	3	3		4	
		Cit	2	4		2	
		Jou	ns				

Appendices 135

Department	Code	Library	% of Holdings	Rank Order Holdings	Rank Order of Use	Rank Distance	DEI
Social Work	098	SoW	7	3	1	1	94
		Cen	78	1	2	4	
		Cit	9	2	3	3	
		AAHD	3	4		5	
		UnC	1	5		6	
		Jou	1	6		2	
		NSc	ns				
		Law	ns				
		Eng	ns				
Sociology	106	Cen	62	1	1	5	79
		NSc	1	7	2	3	
		Cit	14	2	3	6	
		SoW	2	6	4	1	
		Eng	4	6		2	
		Mat	10	3		4	
		AAHD	5	4		7	
		UnC	1	8		8	
		Che	ns				
		Phy	ns				
		Jou	ns				
		Law	ns				

Group III - Humanities

Department	Code	Library	% of Holdings	Rank Order Holdings	Rank Order of Use	Rank Distance	DEI
Architecture	012	AAHD	54	1	1	4	93
		Mus	ns		2		
		Cen	39	2	3	3	
		Jou	4	3		2	
		UnC	1	4		5	
		Eng	1	5		1	
		Cit	ns				
		SoW	ns				
	032	AAHD	32	2	1	4	94
		Cen	35	1	2	3	
		Cit	26	3	3	5	
		Eng	1	5	4	1	
		Mat	ns		5		
		SoW	0		6		
		UnC	4	4		6	
		Law	1	6		2	
		NSc	ns				
		Jou	ns				
	096	AAHD	52	1	1	2	63
		Cen	11	3	2	3	
		Eng	37	2		1	

Department	Code	Library	% of Holdings	Rank Order Holdings	Rank Order of Use	Rank Distance	DEI
English	002	Cen	96	1	1	2	96
		UnC	3	2		3	
		Jou	1	3		1	
		AAHD	ns				
		Cit	ns				
		Mus	ns				
		Law	ns				
	005	Cen	78	1			0
		Jou	19	2			
		UnC	1	3			
		Mat	ns				
		Cit	ns				
		Mus	ns				
		Eng	ns				
	022	Cen	97	1	1	2	97
		UnC	1	2		3	
		Mat	1	3		1	
		AAHD	ns				
		Jou	ns				
	027	Cen	99	1	1	1	99
		NSc	ns				
		UnC	ns				
		Eng	ns				
Fine Arts	011	Mus	100	1	1	1	100
		AAHD	ns		2		
		Cen	ns		3		
		UnC	ns				
	015	AAHD	96	1	1	2	99
		Cen	3	2	2	1	
		UnC	1	3		3	
German	049	Cen	92	1	1	2	92
		AAHD	ns		2		
		Mus	8	2		1	
		Mat	ns				
Human De-velopment	081	AAHD	59	1	1	1	59
		Cen	31	2		4	
		Eng	8	3		2	
		UnC	1	4		5	
		Jou	1	5		3	
	082	AAHD	90	1	1	1	90
		Sli*			2		
		Cen	10	2		2	
		UnC	ns				

Appendices

Department	Code	Library	% of Holdings	Rank Order Holdings	Rank Order of Use	Rank Distance	DEI
Library Science	099	Cen	96	1	1	3	97
		Cit	1	2	2	5	
		AAHD	1	3		4	
		Eng	1	4		1	
		NSc	1	5		2	
		Jou	ns				
		UnC	ns				
		Mat	ns				
		Che	ns				
Philosophy	074	Cen	98	1	1	2	99
		Mat	1	2	2	1	
		UnC	ns				
		Jou	ns				
		Cit	ns				
	086	Cen	94	1	1	2	94
		UnC	4	2		3	
		Jou	1	3		1	
		Cit	ns				
		Mat	ns				
		AAHD	ns				
		Phy	ns				
		NSc	ns				
		Mus	ns				
Religion	042	Cen	98	1	1	1	98
		Cit	ns		2		
		AAHD	1	2		2	
		UnC	1	3		3	
	112	Cen	85	1	1	1	87
		Cit	2	3	2	2	
		UnC	ns		3		
		Jou	ns		4		
		AAHD	13	2		3	
		Eng	ns				
		SoW	ns				
Romance Languages	095	Cen	99	1	1	1	99
		AAHD	ns				
		UnC	ns				
		Jou	ns				
Visual and Performing Arts	016	Mus	99	1	1	1	100
		Cen	1	2	2	2	
		AAHD	ns				
	019	Mus	100	1	1	1	100
		Cen	ns				
	030	Mus	97	1	1	1	97
		Cen	3	2		2	

Department	Code	Library	% of Holdings	Rank Order Holdings	Rank Order of Use	Rank Distance	DEI
Visual and Performing Arts	033	AAHD	95	1	1	2	95
		Mat	5	2		1	
	036	Cen	2	2	1	2	97
		Mus	95	1	2	1	
		AAHD	ns		3		
		UnC	3	3		3	
	063	Cen	86	1	1	7	88
		AAHD	2	3	2	8	
		Jou	3	2		1	
		UnC	2	4		9	
		Cit	2	5		6	
		Phy	1	6		4	
		Eng	1	7		3	
		Mat	1	8		5	
		SoW	1	9		2	
		Che	ns				
	067	Mus	100	1	1	1	100
	079	AAHD	97	1	1	2	97
		Cen	3	2		1	
	087	AAHD	66	1	1	2	97
		Cen	31	2	2	1	
		UnC	3	3		3	
	103	Eng	71	1	1	2	96
		AAHD	10	3	2	6	
		Cen	15	2	3	3	
		Che	2	4		5	
		Mat	1	5		4	
		Phy	1	6		1	
		UnC	ns				
	104	Mus	98	1	1	1	100
		Cen	2	2	2	2	
		UnC	ns				
	107	Fil*			1		89
		AAHD	89	1	2	1	
		NSc	ns		3		
		Cen	8	2		2	
		UnC	1	3		4	
		Jou	1	4		3	
		Mat	ns				
		Eng	ns				
	120	Mus	99	1	1	1	100
		Cen	1	2	2	2	
		UnC	ns				

Appendix B-5

RANGES DERIVED FROM DOCUMENT DISPERSION PATTERNS

RANGES

Group I - Sciences

Total number of libraries housing relevant documents	4-12
Number of libraries used	1-6
Percent holdings - first library used	9-96
DEI	49-100
ER	0-10

Group II - Social Sciences

Total number of libraries housing relevant documents	4-13
Number of libraries used	0-5
Percent holdings - first library used	0-99
DEI	0-100
ER	0-9

Group III - Humanities

Total number of libraries housing relevant documents	1-10
Number of libraries used	0-6
Percent holdings - first library used	0-100
DEI	0-100
ER	2-9

Appendix B-6

Summary of Means by Group and Department: Library Holding Documents, Library Used, Document Exposure Index, and Expectation Rate.

Group	Department	n	Lib. Holding Docs.	Lib. Used	DEI	ER
Group I Sciences	Air Force	1	4.00	1.00	65	8.00
	Biology	2	6.50	2.00	83	8.00
n = 24	Chemistry	4	7.75	2.50	85	9.12
	Engineering	9	8.22	3.67	86	6.22
	Human Development	1	6.00	3.00	77	8.00
	Mathematics	1	7.00	1.00	86	9.00
	Physics	1	7.00	2.00	68	9.50
	Psychology	4	10.25	1.00	69	3.67
	Science Teaching	1	13.00	1.00	60	6.00
	Group Means		8.17	2.46	80	6.96
Group II Social Sciences	Air Force	1	8.00	0.00	0	0.00
	Anthropology	3	8.33	2.00	94	5.00
n = 45	Army, ROTC	1	7.00	1.00	0	7.00
	Economics	3	9.67	3.33	95	4.00
	Education	7	7.86	0.86	69	6.20
	Geography	3	9.67	3.00	95	5.33

History	7	7.28	2.86	95	5.07
Human Development	3	8.00	2.00	92	7.50
Management	5	9.00	2.20	70	4.50
Political Science	3	8.00	2.00	67	3.33
Public Communications	2	8.50	2.00	90	5.50
Social Work	6	8.83	2.67	81	7.08
Sociology	1	12.00	4.00	79	1.00
Group Means		8.42	2.20	79	5.00
Group III Humanities $n = 31$					
Architecture	3	6.67	3.67	83	6.17
English	4	5.75	0.75	73	4.25
Fine Arts	2	3.50	1.50	99	6.25
German	1	4.00	1.00	92	5.00
Human Development	2	4.00	1.00	74	6.50
Library Science	1	10.00	2.00	97	5.00
Philosophy	2	7.00	1.50	96	7.75
Religion	2	5.50	3.00	92	4.50
Romance Languages	1	4.00	1.00	99	5.00
Visual & Performing Arts	13	3.77	1.69	97	6.38
Group Means		4.84	1.75	91	5.91
Population Means		7.25	2.12	83	5.76

Summary of Means (cont.)

Group	n	Total Lib. Holding Docs.	Total Lib. Used	Exp. Ind. First	DEI	ER
I. Sciences	24	8.17	2.46	57	80	6.96
II. Social Sciences	45	8.42	2.20	54	79	5.00
III. Humanities	31	4.84	1.74	82	91	5.91

Appendix B-7

DOCUMENT EXPOSURE INDEX: FREQUENCY DISTRIBUTION

DEI	f
0-ns*	5
1-10	1
11-20	2
21-30	-
31-40	-
41-50	1
51-60	3
61-70	6
71-80	5
81-90	17
91-100	60
	100

*Includes four individuals who did not use any library in the university system.

Appendix B-8

RELATIONSHIP BETWEEN DEI AND LIBRARY USED FIRST-- BRANCH vs NO BRANCHES

		Branch	No Branch
Group I	n	19	5
	Σ	1571	342
	$\overline{X}$ DEI	82.68	68.4
Group II	n	15	30
	Σ	1155	2418
	$\overline{X}$ DEI	77.0	80.6
Group III	n	17	14
	Σ	1567	1245
	$\overline{X}$ DEI	91.18	88.93
Total Population:	n	52	48
	Σ	4293	4005
	$\overline{X}$	82.56	83.44

Appendix B-9

RANKING OF ER MEANS BY DEPARTMENT WITH DOCUMENT EXPOSURE INDEX

X̄ ER	Department	n	DEI
1.00	Sociology	1	79
3.33	Political Science	3	67
3.67	Psychology	3(a)	69
4.00	Air Force, ROTC	2	32
4.00	Economics	4	95
4.25	English	4	73
4.50	Management	5	70
4.50	Religion	2	92
5.00	Anthropology	3	94
5.00	Library Science	1	97
5.00	German	1	92
5.00	Romance Languages	1	99
5.07	History	7	95
5.33	Geography	3	95
5.50	Public Communications	2	90
6.00	Science Teaching	1	60
6.17	Architecture	3	83
6.20	Education	5(b)	69
6.22	Engineering	9	86
6.25	Fine Arts	2	99
6.38	Visual & Performing Arts	13	97
7.00	Army, ROTC	1	0
7.08	Social Work	6	81
7.08	Human Development	6	84
7.75	Philosophy	2	96
8.00	Biology	2	83
9.00	Mathematics	1	86
9.12	Chemistry	4	85
9.50	Physics	1	68

(a) One respondent did not give his ER.
(b) Two respondents did not give their ERs.

Appendix C-1

DISTANCE RANGES OF LIBRARIES RESPONDENTS RANKED

Distance*	Ranking						Total
	1	2	3	4	5	6	
0-50	25	10	3	3	1	1	43
51-100	25	18	10	5	4	-	62
101-150	24	17	10	4	-	-	55
151-200	13	10	5	1	-	-	29
201-250	-	3	3	-	-	-	6
251-300	-	-	-	1	-	1	2
301-350	3	2	1	1	-	-	7
351-400	2	1	-	-	-	-	3
401-450	-	1	-	-	-	-	1
451-500	-	-	-	-	-	-	0 $\Sigma 208$
501-550	-	-	-	-	-	-	0
551-600	-	-	-	-	-	-	0
601-650	-	-	-	-	-	-	0
651-700	-	1	1	-	1	-	3
701-750	-	-	-	-	-	-	0
751-800	-	-	-	-	-	-	0
801-850	-	-	-	-	-	-	0
851-900	-	-	-	-	-	-	0
Over 900	4	1	-	-	-	-	5 $\Sigma 8$
Total**	96	64	33	15	6	2	216

*For actual distance in feet, multiply all measurements by 25, i.e., 50 = 50 x 25 = 1250 feet from office to library.

**Totals differ from number of libraries in straight tabulation of libraries ranked 1-6, p. 96 because libraries which were not part of the university library system were dropped from the ranks. E.g., if an individual's first choice library was a non-system library and he also ranked second and third choice libraries, the system libraries became the 1st and 2nd choice libraries for this distance tabulation.

Appendix C-2

DISTANCE RANGES OF LIBRARIES USED AND NOT USED
(All house documents relevant to interest profile)

Distance*	All libraries used		All libraries not used	
0-50	42		27	
51-100	63		72	
101-150	55		59	
151-200	29		27	
201-250	6		11	
251-300	2		1	
301-350	7		7	
351-400	3		3	
401-450	1		0	
451-500	0	Σ208	0	Σ207
501-550	0		2	
551-600	0		6	
601-650	0		9	
651-700	2		20	
701-750	0		9	
751-800	0		3	
801-850	0		1	
851-900	0		0	
Over 900	5	Σ7	18	Σ68

*For actual distance in feet, multiply all measurements by 25, i.e., 50 = 50 x 25 = 1250 feet from office to library.

Appendix C-3

PERCENT HOLDINGS AND DISTANCE OF LIBRARY-- CROSS TABULATION

Percent Holdings	Distance of library he uses first	
	Closest	Not closest
0-10	5	2
11-20	6	1
21-30	1	1
31-40	2	3
41-50	2	1
51-60	4	5
61-70	1	6
71-80	2	6
81-90	3	10
91-100	14	15
	40	50
No library	4	
Other library	6	

Appendix D-1

OHIO STATE UNIVERSITY INTERVIEW GUIDE I

Name _____ Dept. _____ Rank _____
Campus Address _____ Degree _____

1. When you need material from the library, do you
   ____ go to the library yourself to get it
   ____ send someone else for it
   ____ other (specify) _____

2. If answer b, ask--When you send someone else for it, whom do you send?
   ____ secretary
   ____ graduate assistant
   ____ undergraduate
   ____ other (specify) _____

3. Your requests to the campus delivery service are transmitted by: (Indicate all sources)
   ____ yourself
   ____ secretary
   ____ graduate assistant
   ____ undergraduate
   ____ other (specify) _____

4. How often do you use the delivery system?
   ____ less than once a month
   ____ once/month
   ____ twice/month
   ____ once/week
   ____ more than once/week

5. Are there any special reasons for your not using the delivery system more frequently?
   ____ yes   ____ no
   Comments _____

6. What percentage of your library needs are satisfied by material obtained through the delivery system?
   _____ 0 to 5   _____ 51 to 75
   _____ 6 to 25   _____ 76 to 100
   _____ 26 to 50

7. a Has the new delivery service altered your pattern of library use?
   _____ yes   _____ no

   b If yes, how and why has it changed?
   _____ use more   _____ saves time
   _____ easier to use   _____ more convenient
   Comments _____
   _____
   _____

8. Do you rate this new service as:
   _____ excellent   _____ fair
   _____ good   _____ poor
   Comments _____
   _____
   _____

9. a In relation to your own teaching and research needs, what priority would you give a library delivery service in a time of tight budgets?
   _____ high priority   _____ medium   _____ poor

   b Do you consider it
   _____ essential   _____ luxury
   _____ important   _____ other (specify)
   _____ convenient   _____
   Why? _____
   _____
   _____

10. When you request a specific book from the library through the delivery system, what is your expectation that the book will be delivered to you?
    (0 to 10, with 10 = all the time)   _____

11. a Did the introduction of a delivery system change your expectation rate in any way?
    _____ yes   _____ no
    Comments _____

Appendices 151

11.b If yes, what was your expectation rate prior to the delivery service? (Scale of 0 to 10, with 10 = all the time.) _____
Comments _____
_____
_____

12. For what purposes do you use materials acquired through the delivery service? (Include all)
    ____ classwork
    ____ personal (avocation)
    ____ research
    ____ other (specify) _____

13. The last time you requested a book from the delivery system, were you
    ____ satisfied
    ____ dissatisfied
    ____ don't remember

14. Has the availability of delivery service affected the percentage of documents you are now able to examine?
    ____ yes   ____ no
    If yes, how? _____
    _____
    _____

15. Of the following sources, which ones do you consider important sources of information for your teaching and research? ("Information" is defined here to include bibliographic citations, document retrieval, ideas and concepts, latest research and development in his field, etc.).

	Important	Unimportant
doctoral students	____	____
personal collections (subscriptions, papers, books, etc.)	____	____
university library system	____	____
colleagues' collections (journals, Xerox copies, books, etc.)	____	____
papers at professional meetings	____	____

15. (cont.)

	Important	Unimportant
departmental reading rooms (not part of the university library system)	_____	_____
conversation with colleagues on campus	_____	_____
conversation with colleagues off campus	_____	_____
other (specify) _____	_____	_____

16. Will you please rank the sources you use in order of their importance? (Rank only sources noted as important.)

17. In what year did you receive your last earned degree?
    _____ less than 5 years   _____ 16 to 20 years
    _____ 6 to 10 years   _____ more than 20 years
    _____ 11 to 15 years

18. a Are you currently working on another degree?
    _____ yes   _____ no

    b If yes, in what area? _____
              Degree _____

19. What is your reaction to the following statement: a faculty member should be able to request materials from the library and have them delivered to his office.
    _____ strongly agree   _____ disagree
    _____ agree   _____ strongly disagree
    _____ uncertain
    Why? _____
    _____
    _____

20. What is your reaction to the following statement: graduate students should be able to request materials from the library and have them delivered to them.
    _____ strongly agree   _____ disagree
    _____ agree   _____ strongly disagree
    _____ uncertain

Appendices 153

20. (cont.)
    Why? _____
    _____
    _____

21. If we were to read your publication titles for the last five years, would they reflect your current research interests?

    _____ yes   _____ no

22. Do the courses you taught in the current academic year reflect your current research interests?

    _____ yes   _____ no

Appendix D-2

TABULATIONS FOR OSU GUIDE I

Rank	f	%
Professor	12	20
Assoc. Prof.	5	8
Asst. Prof.	14	24
Instructor	8	14
Lecturer	1	2
Others*	18	30
Unknown	1	2
	59	100

*Others	
Adm. Asst.	2
Student - staff	4
Research Assoc.	4
Teaching Assoc.	3
Fellow	2
Director of support services	2
Prog. supervisor	1
	18

Department

Group I		Group II	
Agric. Economics	3	Anthropology	1
Agric. Eng.	1	Design	2
Allied Medicine	1	E. Asian Lang. & Lit.	1
Chemistry	1	English	6
Computer Science	1	History	7
Engineering	2	History of Art	1
Finance	1	Home Economics	2
Food Sci. & Nutr.	1	Law	2
Mathematics	1	Music	1
Natural Resources	1	Political Science	2
Nursing	2	Romance Languages	2
Optometry	1	Social Work	1
Pharmacology	1	Sociology	1
Psychology	2	Speech Comm.	1
		Other	10
Total	19		40
Percent	32		68

Appendices

Degrees	f	%
Ph.D., Doctor of Law	25	42
MA or MS	23	39
Bachelor	5	8
Less than Bachelor	4	7
No answer	2	4
	59	100

1. When you need material from the library, do you

	f	%	*Others--specifics	
a) Go yourself	31	52		
b) Send someone else	8	14	Uses computers	2
c) Others*	3	5	Calls to see if	
d) Yourself + send someone	11	19	have	4
e) Yourself + other	3	5	Calls for delivery	1
f) Yourself + send + other	2	3	Work study	1
g) No answer	1	2		
	59	100		

Combined Tabulation	f	%
Go yourself (a, d, e, f)	47	79
Send someone (b, d, f)	21	36
Other (c, e, f)	8	14
No answer	1	2

2. If answer b (send someone else), whom do you send?

	f	n=21 %	n=59 %
Secretary	3	14	5
Grad. assistant	5	24	8
Undergraduate	5	24	8
Secretary + grad. asst.	1	5	2
Secretary + undergrad.	1	5	2
Grad. asst. + undergrad.	4	19	7
Other	2	9	3
	21		

Combined Tabulation	f	n=21 %	n=59 %
Secretary	5	24	8
Graduate assistant	10	48	17
Undergraduate	10	48	17
Other	2	10	3

3. Your requests to the campus delivery service are transmitted by:

	f	%
Self	48	81
Secretary	2	3
Graduate assistant	0	0
Undergraduate	0	0
Other	2	3
Self + secretary	1	2
Self, GA, + undergrad	1	2
Self + other	2	3
Self + undergrad	1	2
No answer	2	3
	59	100

<u>Combined Tabulation</u>

	f	%
Self	52	88
Secretary	3	5
Grad. assistant	1	2
Undergraduate	2	3
Other	4	7
No answer	2	3
	64	

Note: $\% = \frac{f}{n}$, where

n = no. of respondents (59)

4. How often do you use the delivery system?

	f	%
Less than 1/month	11	19
Once/month	8	14
Twice/month	15	25
Once/week	13	22
More than once/week	12	20
	59	100

5. Are there reasons for not using it more often?

	f	%
Yes	29	49
No	28	48
No answer	2	3
	59	100

Appendices

Selected Comments:

Personal needs, habits, idiosyncracies--independent of delivery service

> Likes to browse in stacks--"stack hunt"
> Administrative responsibilities--limited time for library research
> "Don't know what I want" or more specifically, what library has
> Wait till last minute--need materials quickly
> Inertia
> Good personal library--buys own books
> Like to go to library--like atmosphere, change

Convenience of other methods

> Near branch library (same building)
> Have work-study student--faster

Problems with delivery service--limitations of system

> Periodicals, reference materials not included
> Have problems with delivery--supposedly sent but not received
> Don't have time to wait--service not fast enough
> If book not available when first requested, won't deliver; must pick up

Problems with on-line system

> Can't do subject search by phone--need better bibliographic access
> Periodicals over classified--include serials, titles that should circulate
> Computer doesn't list books by title known; can't retrieve them
> Like to check holdings in a particular area. Would be nice to have a scanner by LC number. Saves browsing.

6. Percentage of library needs met by delivery service.

	f	%
0-5	8	14
6-25	8	14
26-50	21	35
51-75	15	25
76-100	7	12
	59	100

Note: Some may have referred to "book needs" only. Periodicals not included in delivery system.

7.a Has new delivery changed pattern of library use?

	f	%
Yes	51	86
No	8	14
	59	100

7.b Reasons cited.

	f	%
Use more	36	61
Easier to use	46	78
Saves time	48	81
More convenient	42	71
Other	5	8

Selected Comments:

Use delivery service because it's a time saver. "Fantastic."
Plan ahead to take advantage of efficiency of service.
Efficient. When planning, used to have to spend 2-3 hours at library. Now 5 minutes on the phone and the next day the materials are delivered.
Works very well for me. In past, put off looking for something because didn't have the time. Now easy to pick up phone and ask for it.
Browsing altered because no longer in library as often.
In library less than before.
Much more likely to use the library with delivery.
 Look up things might otherwise neglect. Like having an extra hour or two a day.
Increased use of library books.
Wouldn't be using library without the delivery service.
Use monographs from other branches.
Convenient, if you can wait for the materials. Widens

Appendices

the possibility of library use. More effective and interesting.

8. Rating of the service.

	f	%
Excellent	35	59
Good	20	34
Fair	1	2
Poor	0	0
No answer	3	5
	59	100

Selected Comments:

Excellent	Very efficient.
	Superb.
	Outstanding. Good service; service oriented.
Good	Somewhat slow. Periodicals not included.
	Some libraries fail to send notices that books can't be mailed to you--on reserve, missing, etc.
	The most useful thing the library has ever done. Saves time!
	Once in a while communication problem--otherwise great!
Fair	Too many books not in the system for his needs.

9.a Priority rating.

	f	%
High	24	41
Medium	19	32
Low	16	27
	59	100

9.b Description of delivery service.

	f	%
Essential	8	14
Important	16	27
Convenient	19	32
Luxury	6	10
Essential, important, & convenient	2	3
Important & convenient	6	10
Convenient & luxury	1	2
Essential & important	1	2

9.b (cont.)
Summary:

	f	%
Essential	11	19
Important	25	42
Convenient	28	47
Luxury	7	12

Selected Comments:

Essential	Wouldn't use library otherwise. Time valuable.
Important	Have access to more materials. Saves searching time.
Convenient	Purchase of materials more important. You can do it yourself, but it is convenient.
Luxury	Low use. Would depend upon what else would be sacrificed.

9.a and 9.b Cross Tabulation: Budget Priority and Service Utility

Budget Priority		Total No.	Service Utility				Total
			Essential	Important	Convenient	Luxury	
High	n	24	9	13	7	0	29
	%	41	15	22	12	0	49
Medium	n	19	2	7	12	1	22
	%	32	3	12	20	2	37
Low	n	16	0	5	9	6	20
	%	27	0	8	15	10	34
Total	n	59	11	25	28	7	71
	%	100	19	42	47	12	

10. Expectation rate with delivery.

ER	f	%	ER	f	%
3.0	1	2	7.5	7	12
4.0	1	2	8.0	10	17
5.0	2	3	9.0	8	14
6.0	4	7	9.5	2	3
6.5	2	3	10.0	6	10
7.0	16	27		59	100

Mean ER = 7.62

Appendices

11.a Did introduction of delivery system change expectation rate?

	f	%
Yes	35	59
No	24	41
	59	100

11.b Change in expectation rate since introduction of delivery service.

	Change	f	%
Higher	+7	1	3
	+6	2	6
	+5	3	8
	+4	4	11
	+3	6	17
	+2.5	1	3
	+2	8	23
	+1.5	3	8
	+1	3	8
Lower	-0.5	1	3
	-1	2	6
	-2	1	3

Mean change = +2.56

Selected Comments: Expectation rate prior to delivery system.

Lower ER prior to delivery
   Professionals or trained searchers seem to be able to find things, to track them down better than most people.
   Better control of collection--can call from branches. Economy of time.
   Books are in different libraries. When library searches, does a better job.
   Decentralization of campus made retrieval difficult.
   Books were scattered before; didn't know what branch to go to.
   Low initiative--distance problem.
   More efficiency with computerized system. Know status of books right away. Do not have to go to dozen different stations and end up without the book.

Higher ER prior to delivery
   Prior to implementation, poorer utilization of branches. Now more people are getting their hands on materials.
   A lot of books found in catalog are not listed in computer--at least not so I can find them.

12. Purposes for which service used.

	f	%	*Other	
Class use	49	83	Book preparation	1
Personal	29	49	Course Work	2
Research	51	86	Teaching	2
Other*	9	15	Professional	3
	138		Foundation	1
				9

13. Last time requested a book from the delivery system.

	f	%	$\bar{X}$ ER
Satisfied	49	83	7.82
Dissatisfied	8	14	6.12
Don't remember	2	3	8.75
	59	100	

10. & 13. Satisfied-Dissatisfied with last use and expectation rate.

ER	Satisfied	Dissatisfied	Don't remember	Total
3.0	0	1		1
4.0	1	0		1
5.0	1	1		2
6.0	3	1		4
6.5	1	1		2
7.0	13	3		16
7.5	5	1	1	7
8.0	10	0		10
9.0	8	0		8
9.5	2	0		2
10.0	5	0	1	6
	49	8	2	59

14. Delivery service affected availability?

	f	%
Yes	40	68
No	19	32
	59	100

Selected Comments:

Yes, delivery service has affected percentage of document examined.

> Read more general avocational books--reading for relaxation.

Appendices 163

> Amplified the base of documents greatly.
> Have more time to read because do not have to spend time personally to retrieve.
> I get my hands on more. Don't have to find it.
> Increased it.
> More are accessible with system.
> Increased number I see because get to them now. Before, had a lot of good intentions filed in a drawer somewhere.
> Like to avoid branches. Too far to go. Now call and get it delivered.

No, delivery service has not affected percentage of documents examined.

> Would still examine the books.
> Just made it easier.
> But has changed time frame.
> It's my job to find certain documents. Keep trying till I get them.
> Balances out. A lot I have sent, wouldn't get around to. But don't go to library as much, cuts percentage too. Also, don't always receive what I order. No notice as to why.

15. Sources of information.

	Important		Unimportant	
	f	%	f	%
Doctoral students	26	44	33	56
Personal collections	58	98	1	2
University library system	59	100	0	0
Colleagues' collections	33	56	26	44
Papers at meetings	36	61	23	39
Dept'l reading room	20	34	39*	66*
Conversation--on campus	48	81	11	19
Conversation--off campus	42	71	17	29
Others**	16	27		

*Do not know how many actually had reading room. Question not asked in interview.

**<u>Others</u>

Department current awareness service	1
Other collections--libraries	9
News media--TV, newspapers, etc.	4
Contact with practitioners	1
Gov't and industrial personnel	1
	16

16. Sources of information--Percent ranking

Source	% Rank Impt.	X̄ ranking	% 1st	% 2nd	% 3rd	% 4th	% 5th	% 6th	% 7th	% 8th	% 9th	% No ranking
Personal collections	98	1.86	39	41	14	0	2	2	-	-	-	2
University library	100	2.00	46	30	7	14	2	2	-	-	-	
Conversation--on campus	81	3.76	5	8	19	20	22	5	-	-	-	2
Papers at meetings	61	4.57	2	2	14	10	14	12	7	-	-	2
Doctoral students	44	4.60	2	3	5	10	7	12	2	2	-	2
Conversation--off campus	71	4.78	3	3	7	17	14	17	3	5	-	2
Dept'l reading room	34	5.00	0	5	7	3	3	3	7	5	-	
Others	27	5.00	2	2	8	2	3	2	8	2	2	
Colleagues' collections	56	5.17	2	3	12	5	15	8	10	-	-	

17. Year received last degree.

	f	%
Less than 5 yrs	23	39
6-10 years	19	32
11-15 years	5	8
16-20 years	4	7
More than 20 yrs	5	8
No degree	3	5

18. Currently working on another degree.

	f	%
Yes	25	42
No	34	58
	59	100

19. and 20. Reaction to delivery service.

	Faculty		Students	
	f	%	f	%
Strongly agree	36	61	17	29
Agree	21	36	25	43
Uncertain	0	0	6	10
Disagree	2	3	9	15
Strongly disagree	0	0	2	3

19. and 20. Summary of Comments

Faculty should be able to request materials and have them delivered.

Agree	Disagree
1. increased efficiency	1. not a necessity
2. time saver	

Appendices

Summary of Comments (cont.)

Agree	Disagree
3. greater convenience	
4. more efficient use of faculty time. Increases productivity.	
5. encourages greater use of libraries	
6. cost beneficial	
7. saves time--shouldn't pay faculty to search for materials.	

Graduate students should be able to request materials and have them delivered.

Agree	Disagree
1. saves time	1. should use the library themselves
2. greater access	2. economic constraints
3. greater convenience	

Selected Comments:

Faculty

Strongly agree:

> "Time and efficiency."
> "It's a convenience and an encouragement to use resources."
> "It's easier to use; a cost benefit with better utilization of resources. It provides more information exposure."
> "It's a real asset; increases my productivity."

Agree:

> "A worthwhile service. It keeps stacks in order. Convenient."
> "It's desirable but not mandatory."

Disagree:

> "It's not a necessity."

Selected Comments (cont.)

Graduate Students

Strongly agree:
>"Their needs are not less than the faculty's."
>"Time and access are important to them too."

Agree:
>"Students should be able to have the service also."
>"Seems it's less essential; some merit in student knowing the library."

Disagree:
>"Time is not a factor with students."
>"The logistics of maintaining service is impractical."
>"It's less important; their schedules more flexible. In most cases, they can get to the library."
>"Library good learning experience."

Strongly disagree:
>"Cost factor. It's not feasible."
>"They have more time to do library work."

Cross Tabulation: Delivery attitude--faculty vs students

STUDENTS

FACULTY		S.A.	A.	U.	D.	S.D.	Total
	S.A.	16	15	2	1	2	36
	A.	1	10	4	6	0	21
	U.	0	0	0	0	0	0
	D.	0	0	0	2	0	2
	S.D.	0	0	0	0	0	0

S.A. Strongly agree
A.   Agree
U.   Uncertain
D.   Disagree
S.D. Strongly disagree

21. Would publications reflect current research interests?

	f	%
Yes	39	66
No	12	20
Partially	2	4
Not applicable	6	10
	59	100

22. Do courses reflect research interests?

	f	%
Yes	35	59
No	13	22
Partially	5	9
Not applicable	6	10
	59	100

Appendix E-1

OHIO STATE UNIVERSITY INTERVIEW GUIDE II

Name _____ Dept. _____ Rank _____
Campus Address _____ Degree _____

1. When you need material from the library, do you
   _____ go to the library yourself to get it
   _____ send someone else for it
   _____ other (specify) _____

2. If answer b, ask--When you send someone else for it, whom do you send?
   _____ secretary
   _____ graduate assistant
   _____ undergraduate
   _____ other (specify) _____

3. Have you ever used the campus delivery service?
   _____ yes   _____ no

4. If yes, how often do you use the delivery system?
   _____ less than once a month
   _____ once/month
   _____ twice/month
   _____ once/week
   _____ more than once/week

5. Is there any particular reason why you have not used the delivery system?
   _____
   _____
   _____

6. When you go to the library to look for a specific book, what is your expectation that when you leave the library you will have the book in hand?

   _____
   (0 to 10, with 10 = all the time)

Appendices 169

7. The last time you requested a book from the delivery system, were you
    _____ satisfied
    _____ dissatisfied
    _____ don't remember

8. Of the following sources, which ones do you consider important sources of information for your teaching and research? ("Information" is defined here to include bibliographic citations, document retrieval, ideas and concepts, latest research and development in his field, etc.).

	Important	Unimportant
doctoral students	_____	_____
personal collections (subscriptions, papers, books, etc.)	_____	_____
university library system	_____	_____
colleagues' collections (journals, Xerox copies, books, etc.)	_____	_____
papers at professional meetings	_____	_____
departmental reading rooms (not part of the university library system)	_____	_____
conversation with colleagues on campus	_____	_____
conversation with colleagues off campus	_____	_____
other (specify) _____	_____	_____

9. Will you please rank the sources you use in order of their importance? (Rank only sources noted as important.)

10. In what year did you receive your last earned degree?
    _____ less than 5 years   _____ 16 to 20 years
    _____ 6 to 10 years   _____ more than 20 years
    _____ 11 to 15 years

11. a Are you currently working on another degree?
         _____ yes   _____ no

    b If yes, in what area? _____
                      Degree _____

12. What is your reaction to the following statement: a faculty member should be able to request materials from the library and have them delivered to his office.
         _____ strongly agree   _____ disagree
         _____ agree   _____ strongly disagree
         _____ uncertain
    Why? _____
    _____
    _____

13. What is your reaction to the following statement: graduate students should be able to request materials from the library and have them delivered to them.
         _____ strongly agree   _____ disagree
         _____ agree   _____ strongly disagree
         _____ uncertain
    Why? _____
    _____
    _____

14. If we were to read your publication titles for the last five years, would they reflect your current research interests?
         _____ yes   _____ no

15. Do the courses you taught in the current academic year reflect your current research interests?
         _____ yes   _____ no

Appendix E-2

TABULATIONS FOR OSU INTERVIEW GUIDE II

<u>Rank</u>

Full Professor	8

<u>Department</u>

Anatomy	1
Classics	1
Dairy Science	1
Economics	1
Entomology	1
Geology	1
Microbiology	1
Nursing	1

<u>Degree</u>

Ph.D.	5
No data	3

1. When you need material from the library, do you

Go yourself	6
Send someone	0
Both	2
Other	0

2. If you send someone else, whom do you send?

Secretary	1
Graduate assistant	2
Undergraduate	0
Other	0
More than 1	1

3. Have you ever used the campus delivery service?

    Yes   0
    No   8

4. If yes, how often? (Not applicable)

5. Reasons for not using delivery system.

Didn't know about it	1
Not familiar with service	1
Don't know whom to call-- use a lot of branches	1
Not sure service is adequate	1
No need	2
Not willing to wait	2
Doesn't trust campus mail	1
Wants to look at book; prefers to handle book himself	2
Likes access to stacks; browse	1
Need to use university catalog	1
Library he uses is nearby	1
His department has library collection	1
Relies on personal library	1

6. When you go to library, what is your expectation?

ER	f
4	1
5	2
7	2
7.5	1
8	1
9	1

Range: 4-9
Bimodal: 5 and 7
Mean ER: 6.6

Comments re expectation:

ER = 4   Has problem digging up changes in titles, etc. (e.g., Periodical--National Conference Board now National Industrial Conference Board).
Wants current items--library doesn't have yet.
High theft.

Appendices

Comments re expectation (cont.)

    ER = 7.5 Because of enlarged graduate program, greater demand on some collections. Collection and management uneven. Fine Arts very well run.

    ER = 5 Bindery. (Must be heavy journal user.)

7. Last time you requested a book, were you

Satisfied	2
Dissatisfied	0
Don't remember	0
No answer	6

8. Sources of information

	Important	Unimportant
University library system	8	0
Personal collections	7	1
Conversation--on campus	7	1
Conversation--off campus	4	4
Papers at meetings	4	4
Doctoral students	4	4
Departmental reading room	2	6
Colleagues' collections	1	7
Others*	5	

  *MEDLARS
  Business Research Office at OSU
  Publisher's representative
  Bibliographies from other libraries, etc.
  Materials from supply houses

9. Rank of sources

Sources	1	2	3	4	5	6	7	8
Doctoral students				2	1			1
Personal collections	4	2	1					
Univ. library system	3	4	1					
Colleagues' collections			1					
Papers at prof. meetings		1	1		1		1	
Dept'l reading room				1			1	
Conversation--on campus			2	1	1	3		
Conversation--off campus				2	2			
Other	1	1	1				1	

10. When did you receive your last earned degree?

5 years or less	0
6-10 years	2
11-15 years	2
16-20 years	3
more than 20 years	1

11. Are you currently working on another degree?

Yes	0
No	8

12. Faculty members and graduate students should be able to request materials and have them sent to their offices

	Faculty	Grad. Students
Strongly agree	1	0
Agree	4	2
Uncertain	2	1
Disagree	1	3
Strongly disagree	0	2

12. & 13. Cross tabulation

		STUDENTS				
		S.A.	A.	U.	D.	S.D.
F	S.A.	-	1	-	-	-
A C	A.	-	1	1	2	-
U	U.	-	-	-	1	1
L T	D.	-	-	-	-	1
Y	S.D.	-	-	-	-	-

12. Reasons for agreeing that faculty should have delivery service.

Great, try it	1
Saves time	2
Univ. should provide resources	1
Efficiency of faculty	1

Appendices   175

    Reasons--uncertain
        Unrealistic economically   1
        Question need   1
        System could be misused--thus
            restricting students   1

    Reasons--disagree and strongly disagree
        Can get own   1
        Browsing important   1

13. Reasons--strongly agree or agree that students should
    have delivery service
        "If used doctoral students"   1
        "Nice but a second priority"   1
        "Can library afford it"   1
        "Library use involves learning
            experience"   1

    Reasons--uncertain
        Learning to use library--
            educational process   1
        Not relevant   1

    Reasons--disagree and strongly disagree
        Students don't have permanent
            office   1
        Students should go to library--
            need to know how to use library 4
        Too many of them   1
        Overuse of resources   1
        Students not entitled to same
            privileges as faculty   1

14. Do your publication titles of the last five years reflect
    your current research interests?
            Yes   4
            No   2
            Partially   2

15. Do the courses you taught during the current academic
    year reflect your current research interests?
            Yes   6
            No   2

INDEX*

Academic "stars" 73
Accessibility of library resources 2, 3, 29
    OSU 54-5, 82-3
    SU 31-41, 77-80, 85-6
Allen, T. J. 2, 4, 73, 75
Appointment phone call--SU 98

Bates, Marcia J. 4
Behavioral characteristics of academic researcher 2
Berelson, B. 2, 4, 44, 66
Besant, Larry X. 66
Branch libraries see Decentralization of collections
British Columbia, University of 69
Bruning, James L. 66

Centralization of collections 2, 3, 48, 78-80, 144
Classified interest profiles 7, 16, 23, 25, 28, 29, 72
   construction of, 16-22
   limitations of 22
   sample profile 20
Communication gate keepers 73-4
Courses, classification of 16-8

Decentralization of collections 1-3, 31, 48-9, 64-5, 76-80, 83, 85-6, 93, 144
DEI see Document Exposure Index
Dispersion of materials 2, 4, 25
   SU 31-44, 64-5, 76-7, 79
Distance 4, 7, 29
   measurement of 27-8
   related to expectation rate 65
   related to library holdings 44, 122-39, 148
   related to library use 44-7, 78, 80, 122-39, 146-7
Doctoral students 15, 59
   as communication gate keepers 67, 73-5, 85

---

*OSU is Ohio State University; SU is Syracuse University.

Document delivery system--Ohio State University 6, 7, 65, 81, 86
 attitudes 57-8, 60, 65, 81-3
 effect on expectation rate 49-54, 56
 evaluation of 54-64
 non-users 13-4, 62-4, 174-5
 users 10-2, 14, 156-66
Document delivery systems 1, 4, 76
 comparison of SU and OSU attitudes 60-5, 81-2
 SU attitudes 110-5
Document dispersion patterns 23-7, 29, 37-41, 120-39
 shelf list count of instructions 116-7
 worksheet 118-9
Document Exposure Index 27-8
 related to expectation rate 43, 64-5
 SU 31-7, 43, 77, 80, 122-46
Dougherty, R. M. 29
Durand, N. 16, 30

Ennis, P. H. 2, 4
ER see Expectation rate
Expectation rate 29, 72
 comparison of SU and OSU 49-54
 definition of 28
 OSU 47-54, 65, 79, 81, 160-2, 172-3
 related to dispersion of holdings 43, 47, 140-2, 145
 related to distance 47
 SU 31-7, 47-9, 64-5, 79-81, 100-3

Fishenden, R. M. 66
Flowers, D. H. 2, 5

Hanson, C. W. 2, 5
"Hard" number 18-9, 21

Information, sources of 15, 58-9
 OSU non-users 173
 OSU tabulations 163-4
 SU tabulations 107-10
Information, transfer of 2, 73-4, 76-7
Innovation diffusion 54, 82-3
Interest profiles see Classified interest profiles
Interview guides 13-5, 29
 OSU users 13-4, 149-53; tabulations 154-67
 OSU non-users 14, 168-70; tabulations 171-5
 rationale 14-5
 SU 13, 89-92; tabulations 93-115
Invisible college 2, 73

Johns Hopkins University   vii

Kintz, B. L.   66

LC Card Number Index to the National Union Catalog   23, 30
Library, effectiveness of   3, 4, 79-82, 84-5
   user attitudes   79-84
   see also Expectation rate
Library, importance of   58-9, 74, 80-1, 107-10
   related to document delivery   58, 65-6

McGrath, W.   16, 30
Methodology   6-34
Michigan, University of--Survey Research Center   2, 4

National Science Foundation   15

On-line circulation system--OSU   6, 7, 81
   SU   6
Organizational structure of libraries   1-3, 29, 76-7
   influence on user access   40-2, 85-6

Price, Derrick John de Solla   5
Profile cards   16, 23-4

Reading rooms, departmental   15, 59, 67, 69-70, 75, 97-9
Relevancy of library holdings   2, 4, 24-5, 31-7, 44, 49, 77,
   79, 86, 96, 140-2
   see also Document dispersion patterns
Research interests of faculty--changing   15, 22, 67, 72-3,
   75, 115, 167, 175
Resources, dispersion of   see Dispersion of materials
Retrievers [of books for faculty]   67, 70-2, 75, 78, 84-5,
   94, 100, 155-6, 171-2
Rogers, E. M.   83, 86
Rosenberg, V.   2, 4
Runners   see Retrievers

Samples--OSU   10-2, 154-5
   non-users of delivery   13, 171
   users   10-2, 154-5
Samples--SU   8-10, 93
Searchers   see Retrievers
Shelf list count of document dispersion   see Document dispersion patterns
Slater, M.   2, 4
Subject Headings Used in the Dictionary Catalogs of the Library of Congress   23, 30

Subject interest profiles see Classified interest profiles

User satisfaction 3, 51-4, 79, 82, 103, 111, 162
    factors contributing to 44, 54, 65, 76, 86
Users, expectations of see Expectation rate
Utilization of library resources 3, 47, 65, 67, 82-3
    OSU 54-6
    related to distance 44-7, 78, 80
    related to teaching 67-9, 74-5, 84, 103-7
    SU 31-7, 64, 77, 79, 86, 95-7, 140-2

Voigt, M. J. 2, 5